Villa of the Birds

American Research Center in Egypt
Conservation Series

3

Villa of the Birds

The Excavation and Preservation of the Kom al-Dikka Mosaics

Wojciech Kołątaj, Grzegorz Majcherek,
and Ewa Parandowska

An American Research Center in Egypt Edition

The American University in Cairo Press
Cairo • New York

Photography credits:
Edwin C. Brock: figs. 2, 4, 5, 7, 8, 13, 18, 21, 22, 23, 26, 27, 29, 31, 32, 34, 43, 49, 50, 63, 72, 77, 80, 81, 84; Waldemar Jerke: figs. 9, 16, 17, 36, 37, 40–42, 44, 52–58 (left); Wojciech Kołątaj: figs. 24, 28, 47, 52–58 (right), 61, 62, 64, 71, 79.

First published in 2007 by
The American University in Cairo Press
113 Sharia Kasr el Aini, Cairo, Egypt
420 Fifth Avenue, New York, NY 10018
www.aucpress.com

This publication was made possible through support provided by the Office of Environment and Infrastructure/Environment and Engineering (EI/EE), USAID/Egypt, United States Agency for International Development, under the terms of Grant No. 263-G-00-93-00089-00. The opinions expressed herein are those of the author and do not necessarily reflect the views of the U.S. Agency for International Development.

Dar el Kutub No. 24593/06
ISBN 978 977 416 076 9

Dar el Kutub Cataloging-in-Publication Data

Kołątaj, Wojciech
Villa of the Birds: The Excavation and Preservation of the Kom al-Dikka Mosaics / Wojciech Kołątaj, Grzegorz Majcherek, Ewa Parandowska.—Cairo: The American University in Cairo Press, 2007
p. cm.
ISBN 977 416 076 2
1.Excavations (archaeology) I. Title
930.10283

1 2 3 4 5 6 7 8 9 10 12 11 10 09 08 07

Designed by Sally Boylan/AUC Press Design Center
Printed in Egypt

Contents

Illustrations vii

Introduction 1

1. Archaeological Research Work *Grzegorz Majcherek* 5
   - Topography 5
   - Summary of the Excavations 9
   - The Mosaic Floors 26

2. Mosaics Conservation Work *Ewa Parandowska* 43
   - Condition of the Mosaics 43
   - The Treatment 45
   - Conservation Measures 47
   - Aeration and Drainage 71

3. Architectural and Functional Assumptions *Wojciech Kołątaj* 73
   - Shelter Design and Construction 73
   - Early Roman Villa *Alpha*—Conservation Procedures 78

4. The Shelter Design *Wojciech Kołątaj* 87
Roof Structure 90
Roofing 92
Niche Construction 93
Panel Glass Walls 97
Footbridge Construction 98
Drainage System 100

Glossary 101
Notes 103
Bibliography 115
Index 121

Illustrations

Figures

	Page
1. Alexandria, city center. Location of the Kom al-Dikka site.	4
2. General view of the shelter location, looking west.	6
3. General layout of the Kom al-Dikka site.	7
4. Late Roman/Byzantine Building B, looking north.	8
5. Late Roman/Byzantine Building B, partition wall, looking west.	8
6. Plan of the Late Roman/Byzantine Buildings B and F.	11
7. Late Roman/Byzantine Building F, pavement in Room F2.	12
8. Late Roman Amphorae 4, discovered in Room F1.	13
9. Late Roman/Byzantine lamp, Frog-type, discovered in Room F2.	14
10. Late Roman/Byzantine Amphora 4 found in Room F1.	15
11. Late Roman/Byzantine pottery found in Building F.	16
12. Early Roman Villa *alpha*, plan of existing remains.	17
13. Early Roman Villa *alpha*, limestone cornice found in the courtyard.	18
14. Roman pottery from Villa *alpha*.	22
15. Stratigraphical sequence in Rooms 2 and 3.	24
16. Bronze coin of Hadrian, reg. No. 4462.	25
17. Bronze coin of Trajan, reg. No. 4464.	25
18. Bichrome mosaic α-2, looking south.	27
19. Mosaic α-2, existing conditions record.	27

20. Mosaic α-3, existing conditions record. 29
21. Mosaic α-3, fragment of bichrome *semis*. 30
22. Mosaic α-3, the *triclinium* floor, looking east. 30
23. Mosaic α-3, fragment of the *opus sectile* field. 32
24. Mosaic α-3, fragment of the *opus sectile* bedding. 33
25. Mosaic α-5, existing conditions record. 35
26. Mosaic α-5, fragment of bichrome geometric pattern. 36
27. Mosaic α-5, multicolored field with bird panels. 36
28. Mosaic α-5, fragment of the guilloche border. 37
29. Mosaic α-6, fragment of a scroll and geometric border. 39
30. Mosaic α-6, existing conditions record. 40
31. Mosaic α-6, *emblema* with a panther, showing previous reconstructions. 45
32. Mosaics α-2, α-3 and α-5, after temporary protection. 46
33. Mosaic α-2, conservation record. 49
34. Mosaic α-2, after conservation. 49
35. Mosaic α-2, stratigraphical section. 50
36. Mosaic α-2, lacuna prepared for reconstruction. 51
37. Mosaic α-2, lacuna after reconstruction. 51
38. Mosaic α-3, *opus tesselatum*, stratigraphical section. 52
39. Mosaic α-3, conservation record. 53
40. Mosaic α-3, bedding cracking due to ground subsidence. 54
41. Mosaic α-3, the same fragment during restoration. 54
42. Northern part of mosaic α-3, with ancient repair. 55
43. Mosaic α-3, modern repair of lacuna filled with cement and bigger tesserae. 55
44. Mosaic α-3, part of the *opus sectile* floor during conservation. 56
45. Mosaic α-3, theoretical reconstruction. 57
46. Mosaic α-3 *opus sectile* part, stratigraphical section. 58
47. Mosaic α-3, *opus sectile* fragment before and after conservation. 59
48. Mosaic α-5, conservation record. 60
49. Mosaics α-2 and a-5 before conservation. 60

50. Mosaic α-5, panels with birds before and after conservation. 61
51. Mosaic α-5, stratigraphical section. 61
52. Mosaic α-5, panel with duck before and after conservation. 63
53. Mosaic α-5, panel with parrot before and after conservation. 63
54. Mosaic α-5, panel with peacock before and after conservation. 64
55. Mosaic α-5, panel with pigeon before and conservation. 64
56. Mosaic α-5, panel with two pigeons before and after conservation. 65
57. Mosaic α-5, panel with quail before and after conservation. 65
58. Mosaic α-5, panel with purple gallinule before and after conservation. 66
59. Mosaic α-6, conservation record. 67
60. Mosaic α-6, stratigraphical section. 67
61. Fragment of mosaic α-6, condition documented by tracing prior to lifting of the mosaic section. 69
62. Fragment of mosaic α-6 before and after conservation. 69
63. Mosaic α-7, during cleaning. 70
64. Shelter among the Byzantine architecture east of R4 street. 75
65. Domestic architectural complex. 75
66. Shelter ground floor plan. 76
67. Scheme of the shelter. 77
68. Section of the shelter, looking north. 78
69. East elevation, concept design superimposed over a photograph of the site. 78
70. West elevation. 79
71. Early Roman and Byzantine walls after reconstruction, looking east. 80
72. Southern wall of the Byzantine Room B1, before removal. 80
73. Niche situation within the shelter. 82
74. Section of the shelter, looking south. 85
75. Section of the shelter, looking east, showing the niche with the Panther Mosaic α-6. 85
76. Section of the shelter, looking east. 85
77. Wooden form for southern concrete beam. 87
78. Roof construction. 88

79. Southern beam reinforcement during assembly. 89
80. Moving assembled trusses to their final positions. 91
81. Final stage of roof construction. 91
82. Niche construction, ground plan, lower level. 94
83. Niche construction, ground plan, upper level. 95
84. Byzantine wall set over mosaic in Room 6. 96
85. Niche construction, section 1. 97
86. Niche construction, section 2. 98
87. Building F, dismantled wall adjoining courtyard, eastern elevation. 100
88. Footbridge construction. 100

Color Plates

Eastern part of the Kom al-Dikka site
Mosaics within the shelter: the Rosette, Birds, and Panther Mosaics
Mosiacs within the shelter: the Birds and Rosette Mosaics.
Mosaics within the shelter
The Rosette Mosaic
The Birds Mosaic
Images of birds on the side and corner panels of the Birds Mosaic
Central panel of the Birds Mosaic
Conservator Ewa Parandowska at work on the Birds Mosaic
The Panther Mosaic
Central panel of the Panther Mosaic
Fragment of geometric mosaic
Mosaic floor of the *triclinium*
Fragment of the *opus sectile* floor of the *triclinium*
Southern corner of the *triclinium* with fragments of *opus sectile* and *opus tesselatum*

Introduction

The chief objectives of this project were the conservation, protection, and display of the floor mosaics from the Early Roman Villa *alpha*, discovered at Kom al-Dikka in Alexandria. The remnants of this building offer a unique example of Alexandrian domestic architecture, showing not only the layout, but also the interior decoration within the original architectural context. The set of four mosaic floors offers examples of different decorative techniques employed in the Roman Imperial period. The total area of conserved mosaic floors is almost 110 square meters and is so far the only such permanent in situ mosaic display to be seen in Alexandria.

The project had three complementary elements: conservation of the mosaic floors, construction of the shelter, and landscaping of the surrounding area in order to open up the mosaics to the visiting public. A principal assumption was that the conservation techniques and the principles of presentation had to be integrated. The shift in emphasis from the artifact (the mosaic) to the archaeological context (the building or site) in modern conservation concepts gives the latter equal importance in the preservation of ancient historical and cultural heritage. The choice of conservation techniques and procedures was driven by the decision to treat the mosaic floors in situ, in their original context and by practical considerations of all environmental factors and possible dangers posed by them. The construction of a shelter was absolutely essential to protect the mosaic floors from potential damage resulting from rainfall, air pollution, and mechanical destruction. The mosaic floors can be viewed from a footbridge spanning the area above the level of the ancient floors, thus removing the potential threat of damage resulting from visitors walking directly on the floors.

Now that the mosaics have been conserved and protected, they constitute one of the most important components of the archaeological park, which is expected to be opened on the Kom al-Dikka site in the near future. It is not only a major tourist attraction, but also an important contribution to the preservation of the cultural heritage of ancient Alexandria.

The mosaics conservation project was financed by the American Research Center in Egypt (ARCE) under the Egyptian Antiquities Project (EAP), which is funded by the United States Agency for International Development (USAID). However, some related supplemental work, including landscaping and the construction of visitors' routes leading to the mosaic shelter, was carried out by the Polish-Egyptian Preservation Mission, currently working at the site, and sponsored jointly by the Egyptian Supreme Council of Antiquities (SCA) and the Polish Centre of Archaeology. The work lasted from February 1998 to June 1999. The staff of the project consisted of Dr. Wojciech Kołątaj (project director), Dr. Grzegorz Majcherek (archaeologist), Ms. Ewa Parandowska (conservator), Dr. Edwin Brock (photographer), and Mr. Assam Mradny (civil engineer).

It is our pleasant duty to gratefully acknowledge the generous assistance of Dr. Gaballah Ali Gaballah, then Secretary General of the Supreme Council of Antiquities, and the friendly support of Prof. Michał Gawlikowski, then Director of the Polish Centre of Mediterranean Archaeology in Cairo, both of whom were essential to the success of our work. Our thanks also go to all the ARCE/EAP staff: EAP Project Director Robert K. Vincent, Jr. and EAP Technical Director Jarosław

Dobrowolski, and to EAP Grant Administrator Cynthia Shartzer, for their help in bringing this project to a successful conclusion.

We also owe a debt of thanks to Mr. Ahmed Moussa, our SCA site inspector, without whose efficient assistance and cooperation our task could not have been completed. We would also like to pay tribute to our Egyptian workers (Mohammed Fawzi, Ramadan Abdel Rahim, Assam Mursi, and Ali Abdel Fatah, to name but a few) who have once again demonstrated their talent, professional skill, and capability to perform even the most demanding tasks. Last but not least, we all acknowledge Ms. Iwona Zych for her invaluable help with the English text of this report.

Fig. 1: Alexandria, city center, location of the Kom al-Dikka site. (Drawing by W. Kołątaj)

Chapter 1

Archaeological Research Work

Grzegorz Majcherek

Topography

The site of Kom al-Dikka is situated in the very center of modern Alexandria, next to the main Masr railway station (Fig. 1). Several centuries of accumulated deposits turned this area into a mound, which was raised and modified in the Napoleonic era when a fort was erected on the hill. The site has piqued the interest of archaeologists for a long time, but the first, very limited, excavations at the end of the nineteenth century brought meager results. Later work on the outskirts of the hills was limited to an exploration of the Medieval layers.[1] Regular excavations became possible in the late 1950s after the hill had been leveled. The site, which covers some 40,000 square meters, has been investigated uninterruptedly since 1960 by the Polish Centre of Archaeology in Cairo in close cooperation with Egypt's Supreme Council of Antiquities. As a result of these excavations, an extensive section of ancient Alexandrian town architecture was uncovered, including several well-preserved monuments, mainly dating from the Late Roman/Byzantine period (fourth to seventh centuries AD).

The excavation area covers the central part of an insula (ancient Roman building or a group of buildings standing together forming a block or square) located in the city center, a town block that had adjoined, to its north, the main east–west street conventionally referred to as Via Canopica. The western face of this block reached the main north–south street R5, which runs toward the sea; on the south, it was bordered by street L2 and on the east by street R4.[2] The course of these streets is known from archaeological excavations carried out in other parts of the city. In the fourth century AD, a wide passage, which the excavators have called a Theater Portico, was traced across the insula, thus providing the main north–south axis for the entire complex of public buildings raised in this period.

The complex is dominated by the imperial baths, with their gymnasia taking up practically half of the archaeological zone.[3] In the southwestern end of the zone, there is a very well preserved theater that adjoins the portico. The remainder of the area is occupied by a cistern, public lavatories, auditoria, and stores.[4] In the 1970s and later in the 1990s, explorations carried out east of street R4 revealed parts of a residential district from the Late Roman/Byzantine period (fourth to seventh centuries AD), including a number of buildings (designated A–H)

Fig. 2: General view of the shelter location before the commencement of work, looking west.

combining habitation functions with commercial and industrial purposes.[5] A sizable part of this architecture was restored and now constitutes a permanent element of the open-air exposition (Fig. 3).

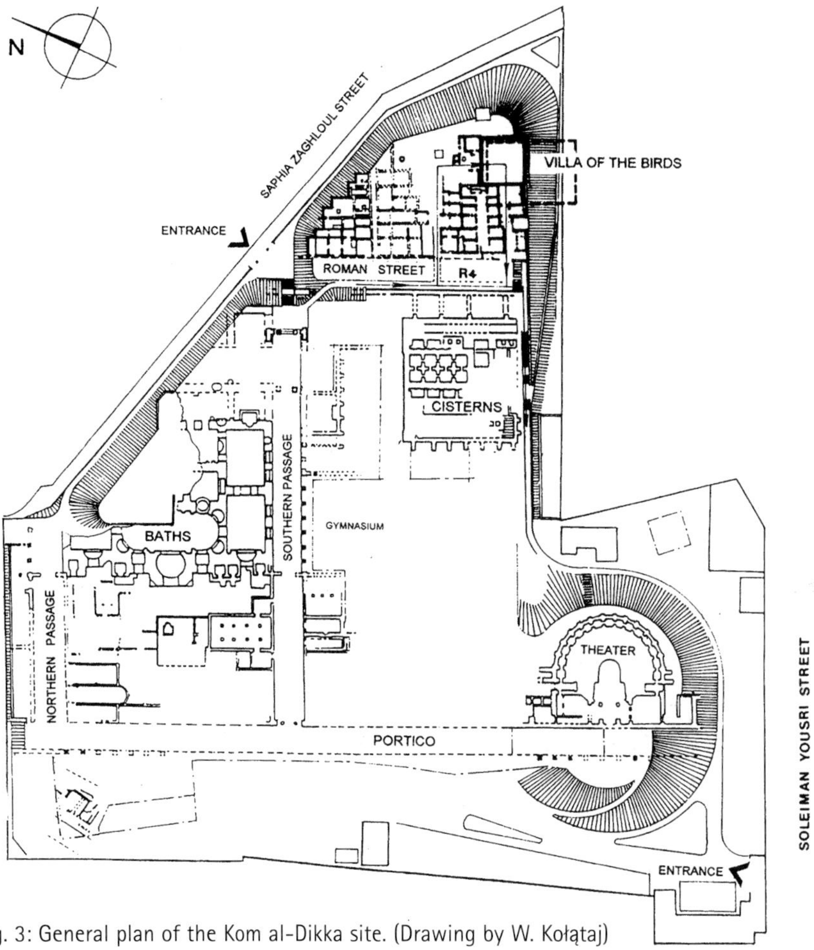

Fig. 3: General plan of the Kom al-Dikka site. (Drawing by W. Kołątaj)

Below the Late Roman/Byzantine buildings, ruins of earlier residential architecture dating to the Early Roman period (first to third centuries AD) were found throughout this area. The site has suffered from systematic pilfering for building material over the ages. Only in the western part of the area have fragments of three urban villas been

Fig. 4: Late Roman/Byzantine Building B, looking north.

Fig. 5: East wall of Building F, looking west.

preserved over a greater surface (designated *alpha*, *beta*, and *gamma* respectively). Despite extensive destruction of the actual buildings, the mosaic pavements decorating the floors in these villas have survived in relatively good condition. The set of mosaic floors excavated includes several examples of different classes and sizes. For a number of reasons—such as their belonging to a single structure, their relatively good condition, and the elements of the surrounding topography—only the four mosaics decorating building *alpha* (also called the Villa of the Birds) were chosen as the focus of the present conservation project.

Villa *alpha* is situated at the eastern end of the excavation area, some thirty meters east of street R4, directly under the Late Roman/Byzantine Buildings B and F. The whole residential district is located some eight or nine meters below the modern ground level. Its borders on the east (modern Safiya Zaghloul Street) and south (fire brigade premises) are comprised of steep escarpments shaped in the course of the excavations, thus there is no way that the work could be extended further. Furthermore, the site is endangered by rainfall running down the artificial escarpment slopes.

Summary of the Excavations

It was essential to carry out archaeological excavations prior to undertaking both the conservation and construction work. The investigations covered an area of some 200 square meters occupied by the Late Roman/Byzantine Buildings B and F together with an interior courtyard and the underlying ruins of House *alpha*. The schedule anticipated a number of work stages, the principal of which started on May 1, 1998 and was completed by July 15 of the same year. This stage involved the full clearing of the mosaic floors and preparation for their conservation. The need to adjust the excavation work to the conservation and construction schedules, as well as new discoveries made over the course of the project (mosaic α-6), necessitated additional work at a later date (January–February 1999).

The first step was to identify the extent of the area and to clear the trenches from excavations carried out in the 1970s. The fieldwork at that time was carried out in incomparably less comfortable conditions, in exceptionally deep trenches reaching in some places a precarious depth of 8 meters below ground level. Most of the work was done in narrow trenches dug in a number of different places, their position determined by the extant remains of Late Roman/Byzantine Houses B and F. Despite these limitations, large fragments of the mosaic floors were uncovered and basic chronological determinations made. Unfortunately, it was impossible at the time to reveal the full extent of the floors, and the architectural context was not completely recognized either. There was thus no opportunity to prepare a plan of the layout or functional arrangement of the building. Following a provisional protection of the mosaics, the trenches were filled in 1974.

The strategy of the present excavation was to some extent imposed by the general work plan of the project. The principal objective was to clear the entire set of mosaic floors intended for conservation. Furthermore, the character of the work required a better understanding of the plan of Villa *alpha*, including tracing the course of the walls and identifying the functions of particular rooms. Another vitally important objective was to collect more evidence for the chronology of the building itself and each of the mosaic floors.

The present work made use of topographical designations introduced in the 1970s. For the sake of clarity, particular rooms were numbered after the mosaic floors decorating them, for example mosaic α-4 in Room 4. A set of stratigraphical context numbers was assigned for documentation purposes. The small-finds register (pottery, coins, oil lamps, etc.) was part of the general site register and followed the rules set down for it.

Late Roman/Byzantine Buildings B and F

In keeping with the project objectives, the first stage of the present work was devoted to exploring the uppermost accumulations, approximately

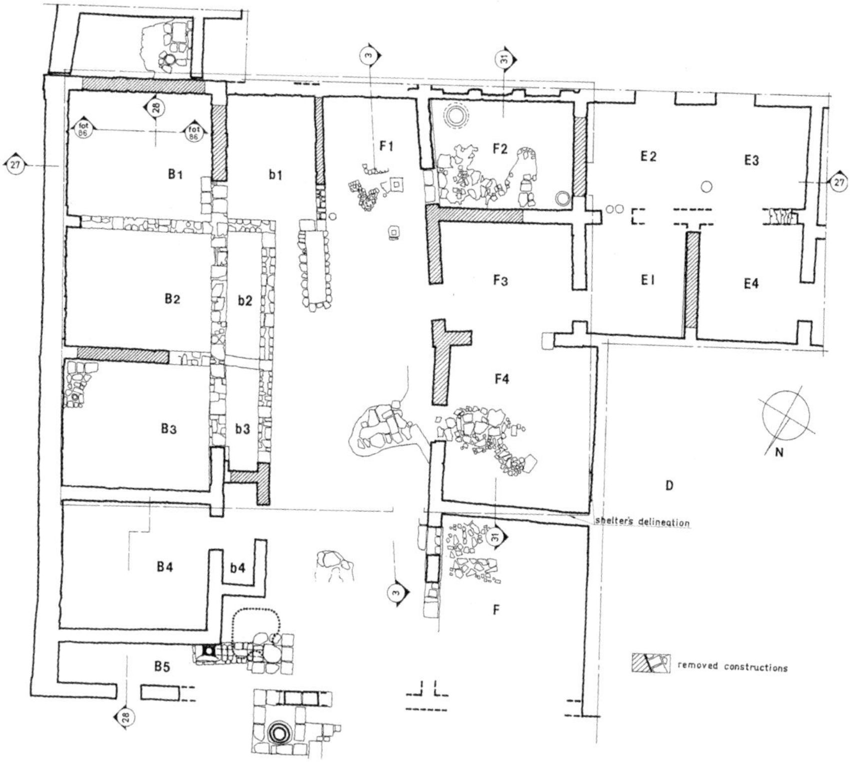

Fig. 6: Plan of the Late Roman/Byzantine Buildings B and F. (Drawing by W. Kołątaj)

1.10–1.30 meters thick, from the Late Roman/Byzantine period, which were integrally connected with the building and occupation of Houses B and F. These two structures, located in the eastern end of the Habitation Quarter, had been uncovered practically in their entirety and investigated in the 1970s (Fig. 6).

Rodziewicz ascertained that Building B, probably used for domestic purposes, was constructed in the second half of the sixth century AD.[6] Its rectangular layout included four rooms of a similar size set in a row. Three additional small units (b2–b4) were added on to the front in the seventh century. The walls of the building survived best in the eastern part, while only the bottom sections of the western elevation and the transversal walls were preserved.[7] Their foundations, made of small assorted stones, brick debris, and furnace refuse, were rather shallow, reaching no more than 0.80–1.00 meters below the occupational level, that is, approximately 50–60 centimeters above the Early Roman mosaic floors.

House F, also used for dwelling purposes and small-scale industry, was separated from B by a small courtyard.[8] It featured a similar layout with a series of rooms opening onto the courtyard (Fig. 6). The walls of the structure were in varied conditions, some rising to a height of no more than 1.40 meters, others existed solely as foundations or even ghost walls. Uncovering the mosaics of villa *alpha*, as well as the overall design of the planned exhibition, required the removal of some of these low Late Roman/Byzantine walls and fragments reconstructed in the 1970s (see Chapter 3).

As both structures had been investigated thoroughly at an earlier date, the present work yielded only modest findings, complementing the previous results. Apart from some remains of the original deposits inside Building B, which yielded no new evidence, the chief focus of archaeological research was on the Late Roman/Byzantine layers inside House F and the western part of the courtyard. In some of the units (F1, F2, F4), the sixth century AD occupational levels were cleared again, unearthing

Fig. 7: Late Roman/Byzantine Building F, pavement in Room F2.

Fig. 8: Late Roman Amphorae 4, discovered in Room F1.

the largely fragmentary pavement made of reused limestone slabs and pieces of marble. The accumulation below the pavement floors, some 1.30–1.50 meters thick, turned out to be considerably disturbed, cut by several foundation trenches and robbers' pits.

The finds from the undisturbed deposits belong to the period of construction and occupation of the house, but equally so to later leveling layers. Just under the floor of Room F1, three well-preserved Gazan (LRA4) amphorae were discovered serving as sediment tanks for domestic refuse and sewage (Fig. 8). All three vessels represent a type produced in the sixth century AD and are quite common in Late Roman/Byzantine assemblages in Alexandria.[9]

Fig. 9: Late Roman/Byzantine lamp, Frog-type, discovered in Room F2.

Other finds originating from corresponding layers included pottery shards. The most numerous group are Egyptian-made ceramics: coarseware, oil lamp fragments (mostly residual), and a relatively large set of amphorae, most of which represent typical Nile silt fabrics. The majority fits into the Kellia 177–179 type series (Fig. 11: 5).[10] A less numerous group is constituted by typical kitchenware vessels (Fig. 11: 4), complemented by a few tiny fragments of Egyptian Red Slip A (Fig. 11: 3) and Egyptian Red Slip B tableware.[11] Imported ceramics, while clearly less frequent, also cover a rather broad repertory of types. A few small pieces represented the imported African Red Slip and Cypriot Red Slip wares, which were relatively common in Alexandria in the period.[12] The imported amphorae collection includes mostly examples from the Eastern Mediterranean: LRA1 and LRA1 *similis* (Fig. 11: 2, 6),[13] LRA2 produced in the Aegean (Fig. 11: 1),[14] and thin-walled, miraculous LRA3 amphorae originating from western Asia Minor.[15]

Directly under a fragment of floor in Room F2, a complete example of locally produced frog-type lamp dated to the second to fourth century was discovered.[16] A few corroded coins from this layer are dated mostly to the mid-fourth century. Based on ceramic evidence, the entire assemblage from the layers sealed by the pavement should be dated to the fifth to sixth century AD.

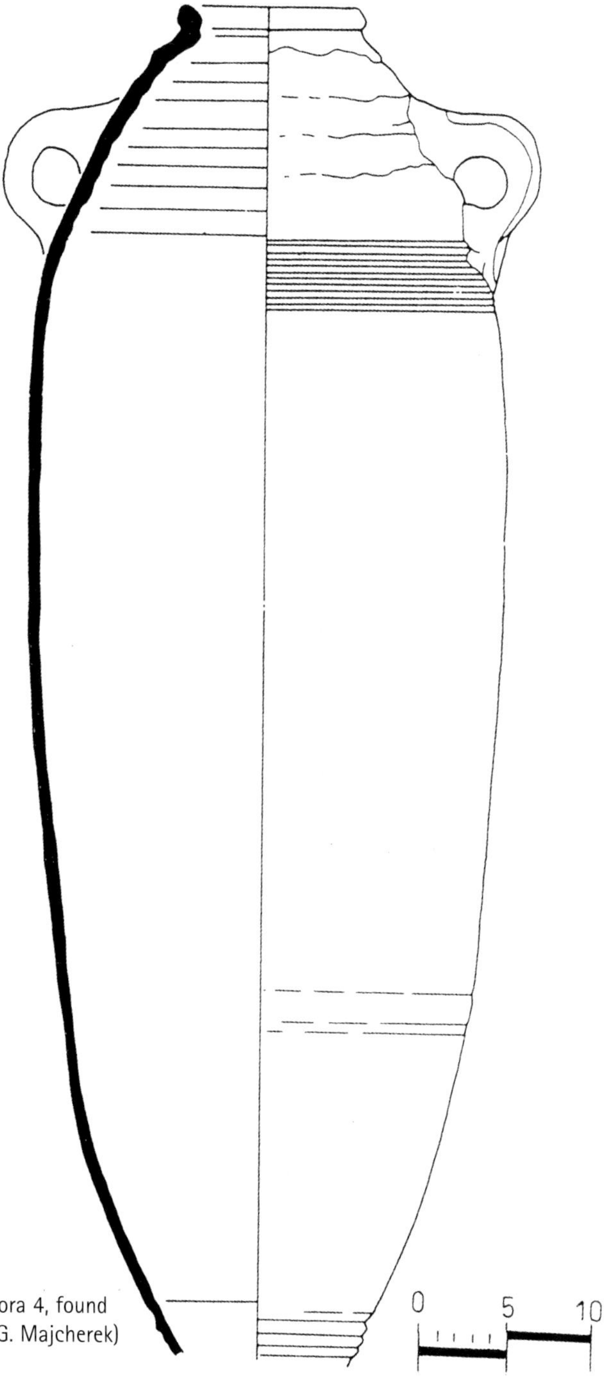

Fig. 10: Late Roman Amphora 4, found in Room F1. (Drawing by G. Majcherek)

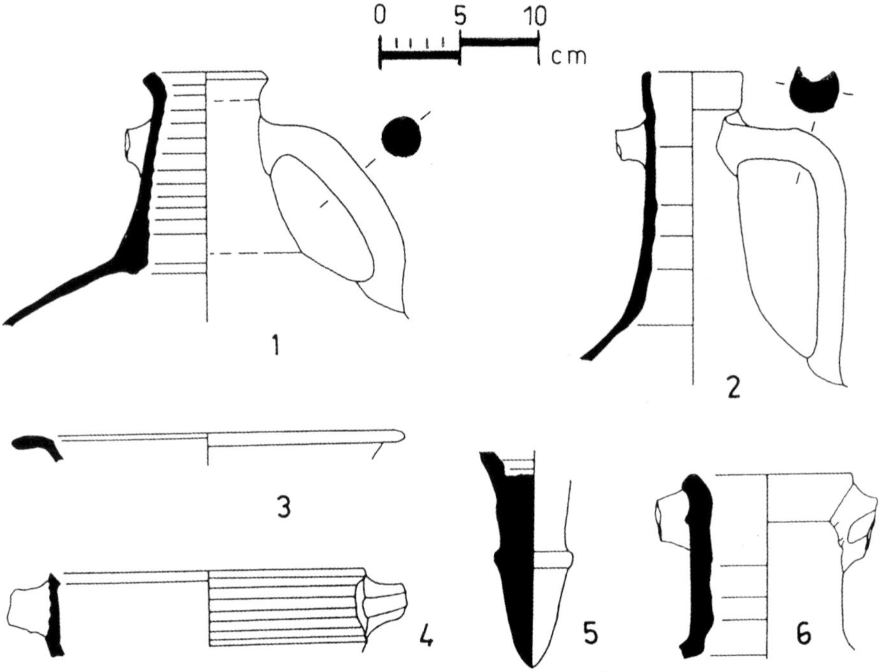

Fig. 11: Late Roman/Byzantine pottery from Building F. (Drawing by G. Majcherek)

Early Roman Villa *Alpha*

Following the removal of the late structures, the archaeological work focused on exploring the layers superimposed directly on the mosaic floors. Undisturbed parts of deposits were accessible mainly in the southern and western part of the explored area. The present investigations led to the complete clearing of four rooms together with their mosaic floors and a part of the courtyard.

Architectural Remains

It was found that the majority of the Early Roman walls had been destroyed in antiquity, either ruined or dismantled for building material once the structure had been abandoned. Part of the original destruction layer of villa *alpha* was investigated in the northern end of the present trench. Below the debris of shattered blocks, mortar, and numerous pieces of painted plaster, excavations revealed only small sections of

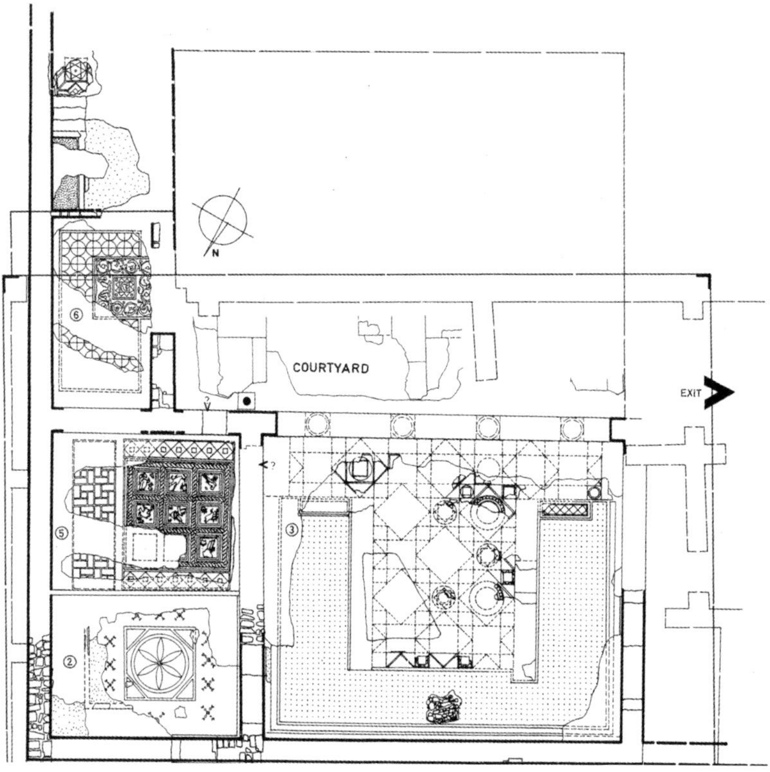

Fig. 12: Early Roman Villa *alpha*, plan of existing remains. (Drawing by W. Kołątaj)

original walls. A segment of a wall (52–55 centimeters wide) dividing rooms designated as Rooms 2 and 3 of the Early Roman villa, was found to run over a distance of 1.30 meters. The blocks in it are partly cracked and dislocated, apparently due to earthquake-related destruction.

Similarly constructed walls (the preserved fragments of which are barely 1–1.40 meters long) were also discovered along the northern side of Room 2 and bordering on Room 3 on the west. The explored sections of extant walls rise barely one course of blocks above the footing, that is, some 20–30 centimeters above the level of mosaic floors. All the surviving structures feature a bond of exceptionally large limestone blocks, sometimes even exceeding 1 meter in length. This kind of construction of *opus isodomum* type (masonry pattern in which horizontal joints are continuous and the vertical joints form discontinuous straight lines) is encountered most often in buildings of the Ptolemaic period, but much less frequently in Roman times.[17]

In other areas (west and east walls of Room 2, north and west wall of Room 6), only sections of the foundations, made of small blocks of varying size bonded in clay, were revealed. The north wall of Rooms 2 and 3 definitely constituted the outer perimeter of the building, as indicated by the presence of another structurally similar wall barely 40 centimeters away from it. The gap seems in accordance with the ancient city law prescribing a space equal to one foot between neighboring houses.[18] The course of this other wall leaves no doubt that it had belonged to a separate, architecturally independent structure extending to the north, most probably another house, designated as *beta* in the earlier excavation report.[19]

Fig. 13: Early Roman Villa *alpha*, limestone cornice found in the courtyard.

In the southern part of the trench, remains of a courtyard pavement were unearthed (Room 4). The limestone slabs were barely 4–5 centimeters thick and originally measured 1.40 x 0.80 meters. A large and well-preserved fragment of entablature found directly on top of the courtyard pavement provides a hint as to the architectural decoration of the house. Limestone fragments measuring 94 x 52 centimeters represent a Doric frieze crowned by a cornice decorated with alternately flat-grooved and square hollow modillions (Fig. 13). Such cornice types of distinctively Alexandrian tradition continue from the Ptolemaic to Roman periods and are comparable to the related second century AD example from Mons Porphyrites.[20]

It appears that the uncovered part of the house comprises only the eastern and northern wings, constituting about a quarter of the original surface area. Neither the overall dimensions nor details of the plan of the building are known, but it should be assumed that in a town like Alexandria, an urban villa layout would have followed all the principles of domestic architecture inherent in the Mediterranean tradition deeply rooted in the cultural and civilizational koine of the Greco-Roman world.[21]

Villa *alpha* most probably had a symmetric foundation, with a main entrance from the south, and a *triclinium* (dining room), marked Room 3, situated on the main axis of the structure. The *triclinium* opening onto a courtyard is the biggest room (7.60 x 6.20 meters). The remaining rooms are significantly smaller in size and their proper functions are difficult to identify. The presence of a small bath in the eastern wing, explored in the 1970s, would seem to indicate that this part of the building served as a dwelling.[22] Room 5, most probably accessed directly from the courtyard rather than from the *triclinium*, appears to confirm this hypothesis. The arrangement of its fine mosaic floor suggests its use as a *cubiculum* (bedroom). The smallest room, Room 2, situated in the very corner of the building and embellished with a black-and-white mosaic, was separated from the latter by a thin screen wall.

Judging by the remains of this room's walls, it had never communicated with the *triclinium*, and must have served as an annex of the *cubiculum*. Room 6 was most probably entered directly from the courtyard, as suggested by the overall design of the mosaic floor, with its central panel turned toward the entrance. Beside the composition of the mosaic itself, this hypothesis is supported by the fact that the courtyard pavement slabs abutted a raised black-and-white mosaic floor α-7,[23] removed in the course of current conservation work (see Chapter 2).

The focal point of the house layout was the courtyard, which provided internal communication and lighting of the rooms grouped around it. Because only a fragment of the courtyard has been cleared, it is impossible to tell whether it was a classic peristyle arrangement or perhaps a pseudo-peristyle. The cornice fragment mentioned above fails to resolve the peristyle issue as, judging by its size, it may just as well have belonged to a monumental tympanum decorating the entrance to the *triclinium*. On the other hand, a typical peristyle arrangement of the courtyard is rather rare in Egyptian domestic architecture of this period.[24] The few known buildings built according to such plan come from Tell Atrib,[25] Marina al-Alamein,[26] and Huwariya.[27] The much more widespread and common *oikos* or pseudo-peristyle layout has many parallels in Alexandria, for example, the tombs of Mustapha Pasha,[28] or other Early Roman houses uncovered at Kom al-Dikka.[29]

Stratigraphy and Chronology

In all the newly explored areas, a destruction layer, varying in thickness from 40 to 60 centimeters, was found directly superimposed on the Early Roman ruins. It consists mostly of stone debris, painted plaster fragments, and a continuous layer of burnt material, including remains of burned beams, wooden door frames, etc. The nature of this layer, considered together with the evidence provided by large sections of the mosaic floors revealing not only traces of burning, but also the characteristic bulges of the cubes caused by the thermal expansion of the limestone ground subjected to high temperatures, leave no doubt that the building was destroyed in a fire. Evidence of this catastrophe is also to be found in the damage and numerous depressions made in the mosaic floors by blocks from the collapsing walls. Numerous pieces of glass windowpane were found directly on the pavement surface.

The layer found directly on the floor surface produced few datable finds. The limited ceramic material from this layer represents mainly local and imported amphorae. Egyptian vessels from the second and third centuries AD are represented—Mareotic AE3 amphorae,[30] and vessels originating from the Nile Valley.[31] Foreign containers include mostly eastern Mediterranean examples: Kapitän II type,[32] micaceous amphorae (LRA3 class, Fig. 14: 3–4) produced in western Asia Minor until the fourth century AD,[33] Cretan vessels of the CA1 type,[34] and a few shards of other containers from the Aegean. Amphorae from the western Mediterranean, while definitely less numerous, are equally varied: shards representing Africana II "Grande,"[35] Tripolitanian III,[36] North African (Fig. 14: 8), as well as Mauritanian types of containers were recorded.[37] The few registered fragments of commonwares include mostly vessels made in the Nile silt fabric (Fig. 14: 9–10).

The fill frequently includes loose tesserae (small stone, glass or terracotta cubes) and even bigger pieces of several dozen cubes. Several of these fragments could be attributed to particular floors, while certain pieces—made of larger tesserae set in a thick substructure—suggest the presence of yet another kind of mosaic floor, possibly from the upper floor of the structure.

The available evidence indicates that the house must have been destroyed in the late third century AD. This event can presumably be linked to the destruction of sections of the town either as a result of disturbances during the reign of Aurelian, or during a long siege of the town by Diocletian.[38]

The fourth century saw a systematic plundering of the ruins for building material and the destruction of the *opus sectile* (mosaic floor

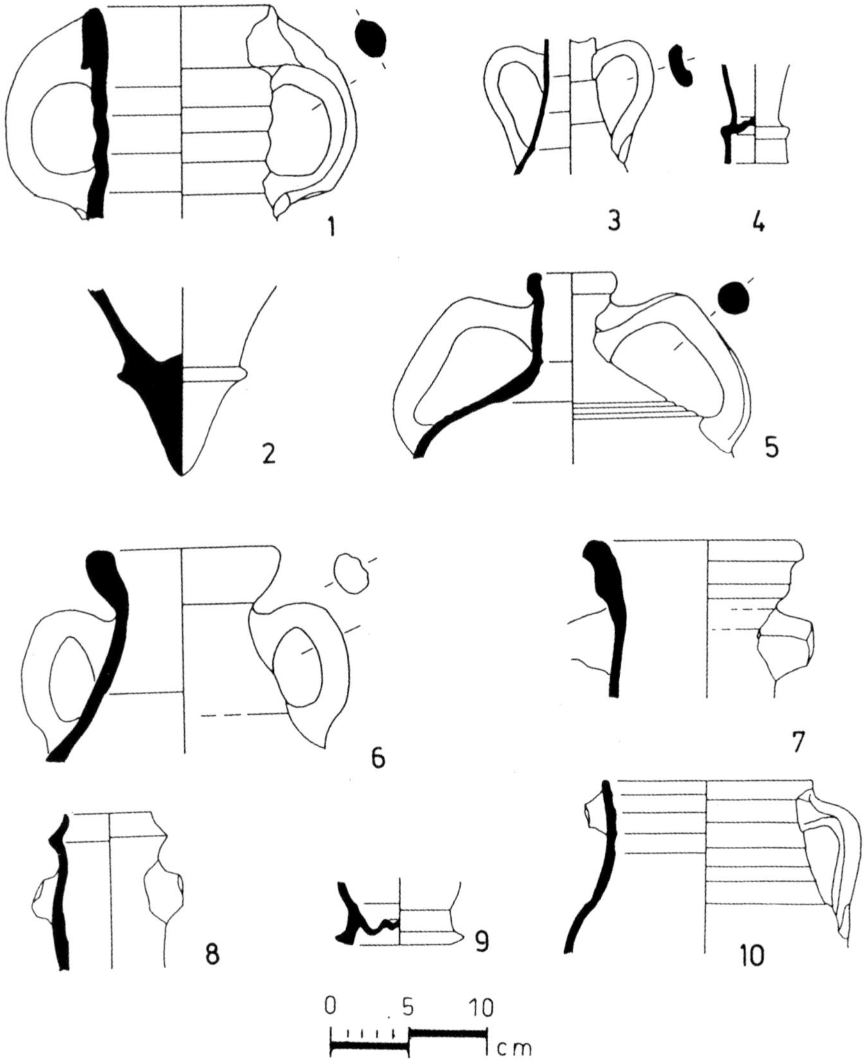

Fig. 14: Roman pottery from Villa *alpha*. (Drawing by G. Majcherek)

execution technique using stone slabs cut to different shapes and sizes, arranged in ornamental patterns) floor. Finds from the fill of a big robbers' pit taking up most of the central part of the *triclinium* (Room 3) and from the destruction layer yielded some fourth century AD finds confirming the suggested chronology. The assemblage consisted of mostly Egyptian wares and imported amphorae belonging to this chronological horizon, as well as one much-corroded coin of Diocletian.

While estimates of the end of occupation of Villa *alpha* are supported by ample evidence, the beginning of its construction is much more vague. Rodziewicz dated its origins to the middle of the first century AD.[39] The stratigraphy of layers under the mosaic floors suggests that the building was occupied for a rather long period of time and underwent a variety of transformations that were basically limited to changes in the decoration and some minor adaptations of the layout. Under all the investigated mosaics, a lime floor from the initial phase of the structure was identified. This floor level was usually placed approximately 20–40 centimeters below the mosaic level. The best illustration of the complicated architectural history of the villa and its relative chronology is the sequence of plaster coating surviving on the wall dividing Rooms 2 and 3 and the series of corresponding occupational levels identified below the mosaic floors (Fig. 15). The earliest of these is a lime floor attested in Room 3, approximately 50 centimeters below the mosaic floor (Fig. 15: 5). The wall decoration connected with it (only the lowermost part has been preserved) consists of a bottom band painted white, separated from the surmounting red band by a narrow, 3 centimeter thick molded strip (Fig. 15: 10), thus resembling closely the First Pompeian (Masonry) Style.[40]

In the next sub-phase, but still on the same occupational level, the wall was repainted with a black dado at the bottom. The next red-painted lime floor, laid some 30 centimeters higher, was found immediately under the *opus tesselatum* (mosaic floor execution technique using small cubes arranged in geometric or figural motifs and patterns) bedding (Fig. 15: 13). The accompanying wall plaster was also painted red (Fig. 15: 9). Similar phasing was revealed in the adjoining Room 2, where remnants of an earlier floor and plastering, albeit much more modest, were also recorded.

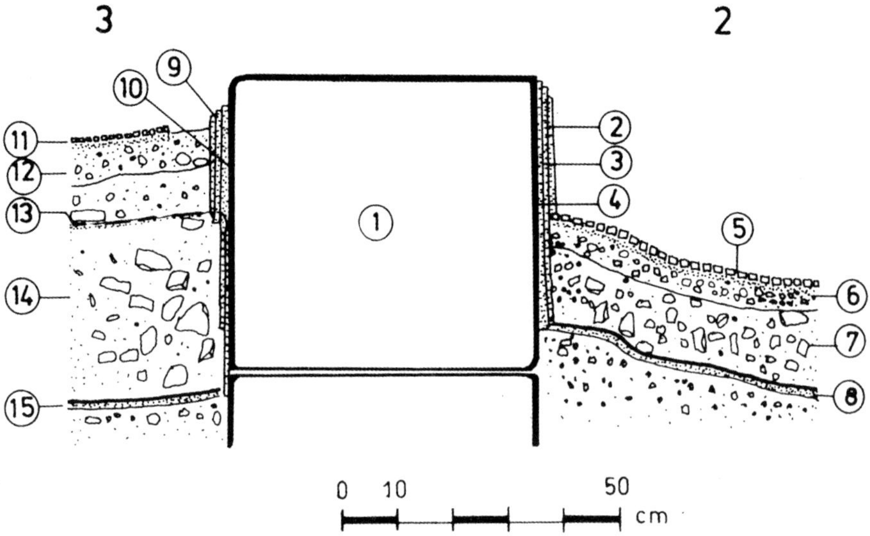

Fig. 15: Stratigraphic sequence in Rooms 2 and 3. (Drawing by G. Majcherek)

1. Wall between Rooms 2 and 3;
2. Outer plaster layer in Room
3. Middle plaster layer in Room 2 corresponding with floor 8;
4. First plaster layer in Room 2 corresponding with floor 8;
5. Mosaic α-2;
6. Bedding of mosaic α-2;
7. Rudus composed of stone rubble;
8. Earlier lime floor;
9. Outer plaster layer in Room 3 corresponding with Floor 13;
10. First plaster layer corresponding with Floor 15;
11. Mosaic α-3;
12. Bedding of mosaic α-3;
13. Earlier lime floor;
14. Fill;
15. Earlier lime floor.

The lower lime floor, in all likelihood contemporary with floor 15, had two corresponding plaster coatings (Fig. 15: 8; 3–4). Contrary to Room 3, however, no subsequent higher level of lime floor was recorded here. A black-and-white mosaic (α-2) was apparently introduced in its place during a subsequent renovation. Unfortunately, the limited scope of the exploration, owing to the fact that the mosaics were not removed, yielded few datable finds that could help to assign a date to particular stages in the development of this house.

Based on available evidence, it should be assumed that the original occupational level of the house consisted of lime floors. An analysis of the sequence of floors indicates that mosaic pavement α-6 was the first to appear, functioning together with lime floors in the other rooms at this time. In the next phase, mosaic floors were installed in Rooms 2, 3, and 5, although it seems that mosaic α-2 slightly predates the introduction of the *sectile* floor in the *triclinium*. In the latest phase, a new mosaic (α-7) was laid on a higher level in Room 6. The courtyard pavement covering an older floor also dates from this time. Some additional light on the date of the mosaic floors is shed by several datable artifacts found in the layers sealed with mosaics. Pieces of amphorae cut to size and constituting the substructure for the *opus sectile* floor consist mainly of sub-Koan amphora of the Dr.5 class,[41] and African vessels, both types widespread in the second century AD.

Other finds also confirm such a dating. Beside an obviously too early and hence residual piece of Eastern Sigillata A plate from Augustan times, a bronze coin of Hadrian from AD 132–133 was discovered under the mosaic α-2 (Fig. 16), yielding a convenient *terminus post quem* (earliest possible date that an artifact could have been deposited).[42] The layer sandwiched between mosaic floors 6 and 7 produced another coin struck by Trajan (Fig. 17).[43] It should be assumed, therefore, that most

Fig. 16: Bronze coin of Hadrian, reg. No. 4462.

Fig. 17: Bronze coin of Trajan, reg. No. 4464.

of the mosaics in Villa *alpha* came into existence in the first half of the second century AD. Mosaic α-6 appears to be slightly earlier and may even have been executed at the very end of the first or beginning of the second century AD.

Thus, the rich mosaic floor decoration of the house can probably be connected with the period of building activity and development in Alexandria during the reign of Hadrian (AD 117–138).[44]

The Mosaic Floors

The mosaic floors, which were the subject of the conservation project, have already been published preliminarily, either fully, as in the case of α-2 and α-5, or in part, as for α-3 and α-6.[45] Hence, we will offer only a brief description here, limited to the essential details of composition, ornamental motifs and colors, with special attention to the newly discovered elements (*opus sectile* pavement α-3, and central panel of mosaic α-6). The method employed is based on internationally used descriptive codes.[46] The mosaic technology, stratigraphical analysis of the substructure and a detailed technical description of the floor's condition will be presented in Chapter 2.

Mosaic α-2

A bichrome *opus tesselatum* mosaic (Fig. 18) originally took up most, if not all, of Room 2 (an area of 2.90 x 4 meters). As a consequence of the present work, the hitherto unexplored central fragment and the north-western corner were uncovered, a total of about 1.8 meters in area. The main decorative element, a sexfoil rosette[47] inscribed in a circle 1.22 meters in diameter with a 6 centimeter border,[48] occupies the center space. The circle is framed by a large square (approximately 1.52 x 1.52 meters) formed of a triple black filet.[49] The corners of the square are additionally cut off by similar black filets turning the inside field into an octagon.[50]

Small black crosslets constitute an additional decorative element, presumably spaced around the central square: bigger ones on the northern

Fig. 18: Bichrome mosaic α-2, looking south.

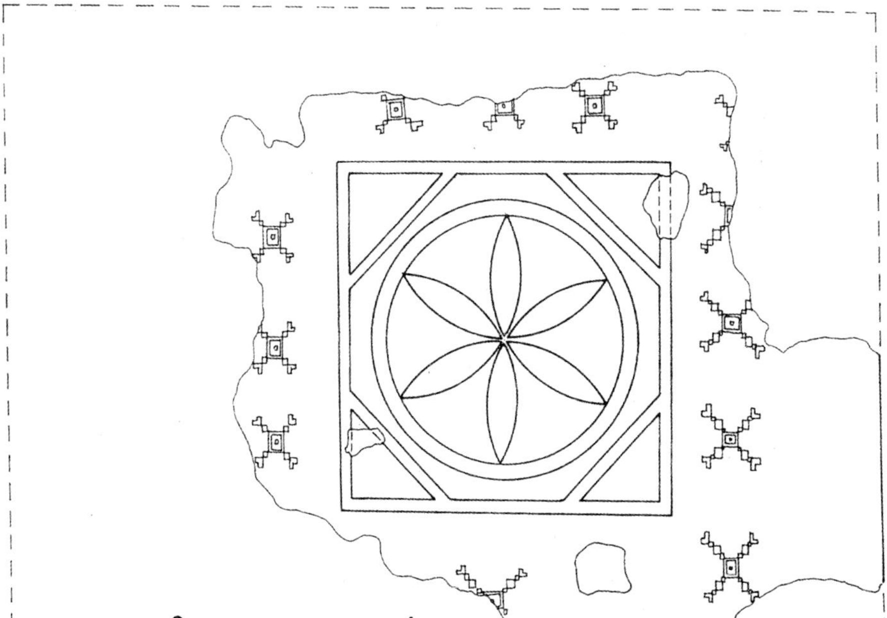

Fig. 19: Mosaic α-2, existing conditions record. (Drawing by G. Majcherek)

and western sides, slightly smaller ones on the south and east. The crosslets are formed of a quincunx of squares, the central square (5 x 5 centimeters) additionally marked by a black teaser, larger than the four other squares at each of its corners.[51] Arms terminate in out-turned chevrons of three poised tesserae.[52] A similar motif, but on a slightly bigger scale, is found on another mosaic, originating also from an Early Roman house uncovered under the Theater Portico and dated to the beginning of the second century AD.[53]

The mosaic is made of medium-size tesserae (approximately 1–1.5 x 1.5–2.5 centimeters) with a density approaching about 40–43 cubes per square decimeter.[54]

The design of this mosaic, utilizing the circle-inscribed-in-square motif, was one of the most popular ornaments found on Roman mosaic floors from Egypt.[55] The coin of Hadrian excavated from under this floor, as mentioned above, dates mosaic α–2 to no earlier than circa AD 133.

Mosaic α-3

The biggest improvements on the previous state of knowledge concern the mosaic floor in Room 3. While only a small part from the eastern edge of this floor, not exceeding seven square meters, had been excavated previously,[56] it was now possible to clear the whole room, thanks to a considerable extension of the trenches to the west (Fig. 11). It was found that the whole room measuring approximately 7.50 x 6.20 meters was decorated with a mosaic floor. (Fig. 20). The composition consisted of two fields, *opus tesselatum* and *opus sectile*, forming the U+T design so typical of Early Roman *triclinia*.[57]

The *tesselatum* mosaic border running alongside three of the walls presents a plain carpet decorated with *semis* (orthogonal composition consisting of repeated ornamental elements that are not adjoining, but appear at regular intervals) of black crosslets formed by four poised tesserae set as saltires[58] on a neutral white background made in parallel rows of tesserae forming a zigzag pattern.[59] The entire field is framed

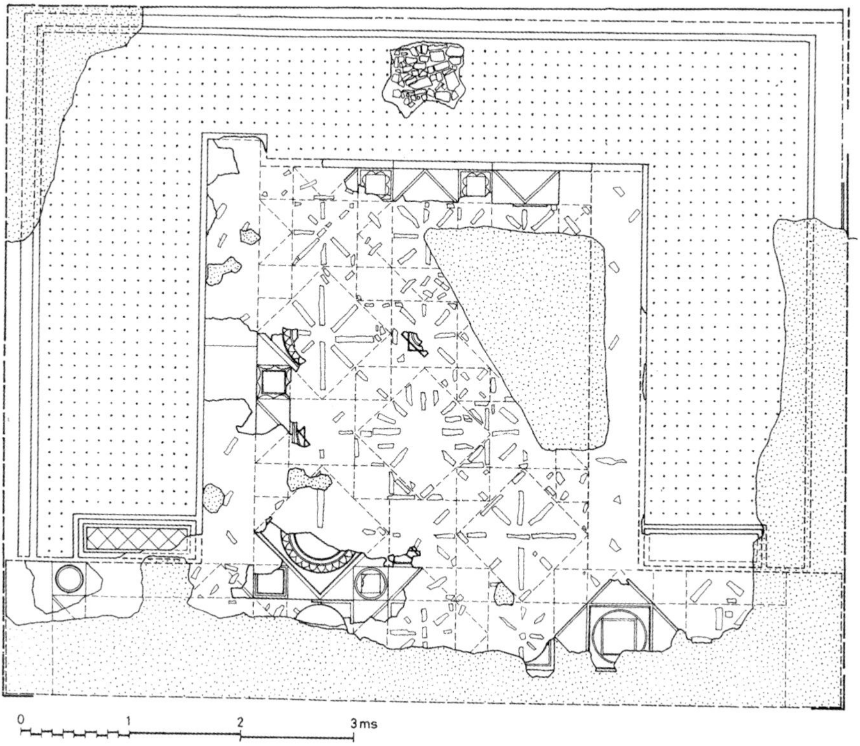

Fig. 20: Mosaic α-3, existing conditions record. (Drawing by W. Kołątaj)

by a double white filet.[60] Inner edges on the long sides of the floor are framed by a black band of four rows of black tesserae.[61] The northern arm of the mosaic directly abuts the *opus sectile* floor. On the outer side, alongside the walls the border is made of two bands of six and eight rows of black tesserae, 6 centimeters and 9 centimeters wide, respectively, framing a wide band of eleven white tesserae. The border which presumably edged the entire mosaic is preserved only fragmentarily along its northern and eastern edge. The two parallel arms of the carpet end in narrow rectangles framed by a black band of four rows of tesserae (4 centimeters wide) around it. Inside the rectangle, enclosed in black triple filet, there is a row of five tangent poised black squares.[62] The width of this mosaic floor reaches 1.40 meters in the back (northern) part and

Fig. 21: Mosaic α-3, fragment of bichrome *semis*.

Fig. 22: Mosaic α-3, the *triclinium* floor, looking east.

1.80 meters in the two symmetric arms; hence, the space is sufficient for the couches used during feasts, leaving free passage behind them.

The carpet was made of small, tightly fitted tesserae, with a density of about 110 cubes per square decimeter. Both black and white framing bands were made of slightly bigger tesserae with a density of 72–75 tesserae per square decimeter.

The uniform and well-balanced tessellated floor constitutes an intended contrast for the lively and colorful design of the central field executed in the *opus sectile* technique, which was undoubtedly the main ornamental feature of the *triclinium*, emphasizing the fineness of the arrangement as a whole. Unfortunately, the *opus sectile* pavement is quite damaged. Apart from some small fragments near the center, remnants have been preserved solely in the western and southern parts of the room. Nonetheless, clearly discernible traces of the particular pieces impressed in the bedding permit a very precise reconstruction of the design. In the area where the marble slabs had been ripped off, the substructure of oblong pieces of cut amphora shards survives in excellent condition (Fig. 23). The fine arrangement of these shards corresponds exactly to the design planned by the mosaic artisans.[63] The basic underlying pattern of this strictly geometrical pavement conforms generally to that of *Décor Pl. 142g*, and is based upon a medium-size module of one Roman foot (29.6 centimeters). Virtually all of the principal decorative patterns appearing in the composition of this pavement are part of a typical repertoire used in the decoration of this kind of floor from the first to the sixth century AD. Nine big panels set at an oblique angle form the dominating element of the composition. Four with the most elaborate pattern are arranged in the main field of the pavement. They contain inscribed discs surrounded with wreaths consisting of white cordiform motifs. Inside each of the discs, there are further rings of black and white lines. The remaining panels are arranged on the main line of symmetry and on a transversal band of *opus sectile* (top of the T-shaped element, adjoining the *triclinium* entrance); the pattern they display is somewhat less elaborate. Each presents an

Fig. 23: Mosaic α-3, fragment of *opus sectile* field.

inscribed square and a circle with yet another inscribed square. The intervening spaces filling the mosaic pavement contain an orthogonal pattern of medium-sized squares. While only a few fragmentary motifs have been preserved, it is safe to assume that they all repeated the same composition. Each contained an eight-pointed linear star in a yellow circle and concentric black rings. The remaining space on the floor was filled with combinations of alternating triangles and squares containing inscribed discs. The lateral edges of the *sectile* floor were bordered with approximately 30 centimeter wide bands of plain gray marble slabs.

Ten slabs used for this pavement represented a variety of contrasting materials: Proconessian marble, green and red porphyry, *pavonazzetto*, *giallo antico*, *rosso antico*, white marble, and local limestone.[64] The impressions left by now missing slabs leave no doubt that some of the elements had been reused and could have come from an earlier *opus sectile* floor.

Despite an obvious symmetry and harmony of design, some inaccuracies and irregularities can be observed in the fitting together of the two

Fig. 24: Mosaic α-3, fragment of the *opus sectile* bedding.

different kinds of mosaic floors. On the side of the *sectile* field panel there are clear traces of the mosaic being cut to size and the resulting damages being repaired. Also, the black band limiting the marble floor on the west is slightly longer than its eastern counterpart. It is not clear, however, whether these inaccuracies represent subsequent construction phases or simply suggest different teams of artisans employed for two separate tasks.

Traces of ancient repairs can be observed in both floors. In the northern arm of the tessellated mosaic there is a fairly big lacuna (about 50 x 60 centimeters) filled with small, assorted pieces of marble tiles. Similar interventions are discernible also in the surviving parts of the *sectile* mosaic floor. A destroyed fragment of one of the squares was filled with marble tiles of a different color and size, interrupting the precise original design.

Mosaic floors decorating Early Roman *triclinia* are not rare in Alexandria. A similar composition design combining a U-shaped border with a T-shaped decorated field can be found also on another color mosaic from Kom al-Dikka, discovered inside the Early Roman House F.[65]

The same design is repeated in the excellently preserved mosaic with a central gorgoneion panel unearthed during rescue excavations at the Theater Diana site.[66] However, all these examples were executed as tessellated floors, although the geometric decoration of the latter seems to refer to the *sectile* models.[67]

The *triclinium* mosaic from Villa *alpha* is distinguished mainly by the use of two different techniques: *sectile* and *tesselatum*. The infrequent examples of *opus sectile* mosaic floors from Egypt do not represent similar designs,[68] but close parallels are present in North Africa and Cyrenaica. The nearest analogy to this decoration system combining two different techniques is seen in pavements from the *triclinium* at the Palazzo delle Colonne[69] and *triclinium* at the "Roman Villa" in Ptolemais.[70] A similar system of decoration can be also seen in pavements discovered at the House of Giasone Magno in Cyrene,[71] and in Building "W" in Berenice.[72] The House of the Cascade in Utica offers yet another example.[73]

The second century dating for *sectile* floor α–3, suggested by Rodziewicz, appears to be further corroborated by new archaeological evidence.

Mosaic α–5

A polychrome tessellated floor (Fig. 25). The composition consisted of juxtaposed surfaces (*Répertoire*, no. IIIb1): a bichrome field of geometric decoration in the eastern end of the room and the main polychrome paneled field with extensions (*Répertoire*, no. IIIb3) framed by a triple black filet (4 centimeters wide). The bichrome rectangular field (Fig. 26), running lengthwise north–south across the room (originally about 3.10 x 0.95 meters), is separated from the main polychrome field by a wide band of fifteen rows of white tesserae (15 centimeters wide). The field is decorated with an orthogonal pattern of adjacent squares formed by four rectangles around a small square creating an effect of interlaced bands ('four-oblong squares' pattern).[74] The pattern is outlined in black double filets.

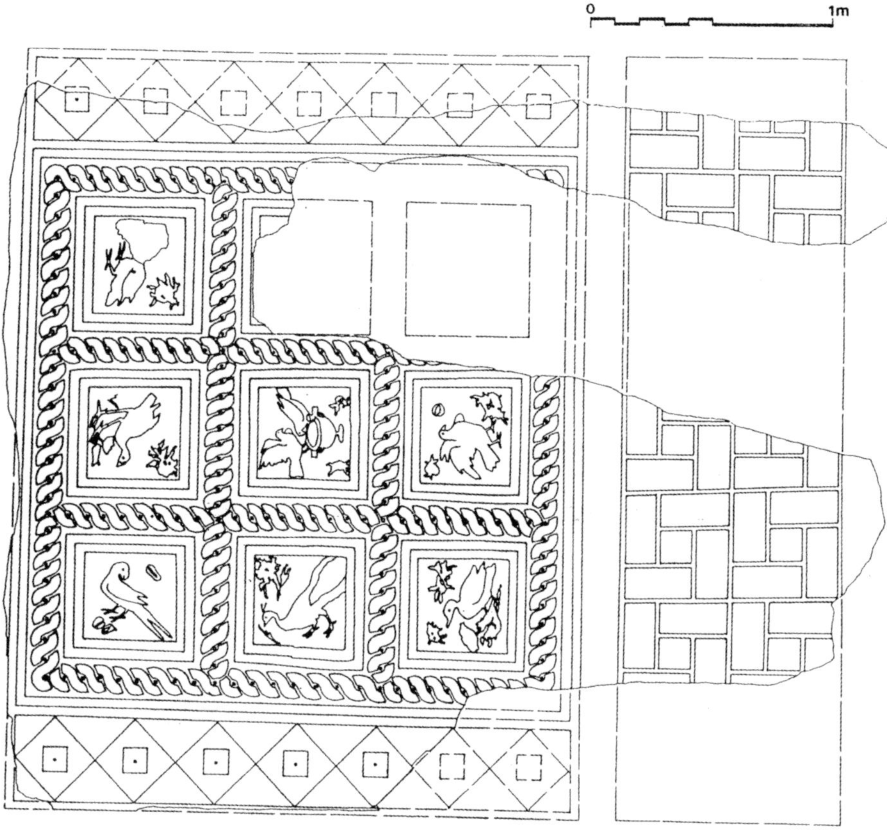

Fig. 25: Mosaic α-5, existing conditions record. (Drawing by W. Kołątaj)

Bordering the rectangular field from the east there is a stretch (preserved 16 centimeters wide) of white tesserae. The density of tesserae used in this part of the pavement approaches 65 cubes per square decimeter.

The main polychrome field forms a square (2.26 x 2.26 meters)[75] framed by a double white filet and divided into nine square panels. Panels are separated from each other by a tightly braided, asymmetrically shaded simple guilloche on a black ground.[76]

The squares, measuring approximately 45 centimeters square, are framed from the outside to the inside by a triple white filet and a triple black filet, both 4 centimeters wide (Fig. 28).

Fig. 26: Mosaic α-5, fragment of bichrome geometric pattern.

Fig. 27: Mosaic α-5, multicolored field with bird panels.

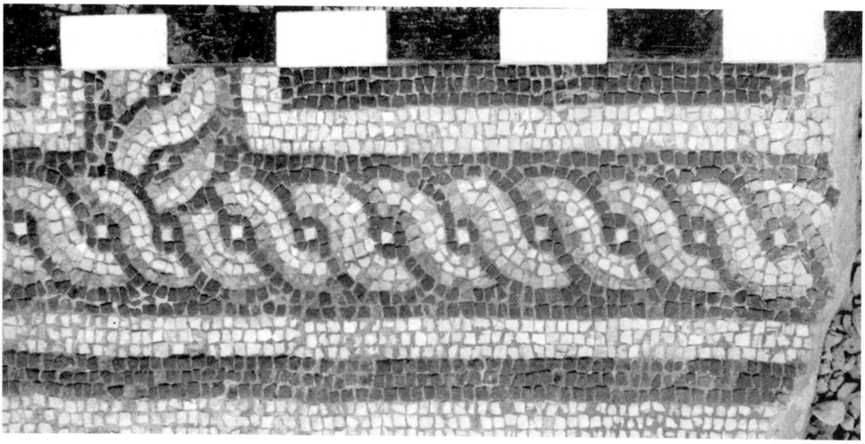

Fig. 28: Mosaic α-5, fragment of the guilloche border.

Each of the seven surviving panels depicts a different bird species on a white background: quail (or partridge), parrot, purple gallinule,[77] duck (Teal),[78] peacock, and pigeons (Figs. 52-58). Shown in the central panel are two pigeons drinking from a *kantharos* (Fig. 56). The departure from the inevitable schematism of pattern-book designs is emphasized by introduction of various space-filling elements into backgrounds of each panel: pomegranates, leaves, and flower buds. The extensions flanking the paneled field are framed by triple black filets. Decoration consists of a row of seven tangent poised black squares. Each square contains an additional small white square[79] whose center is marked by a single black tessera.

The mosaic has now been uncovered in its entirety, with the newly cleared sections including a narrow band on the eastern side and part of the frame around the bird panels to the west. The northern part of the floor is seriously damaged: two of the figural panels and an adjacent section of extension, as well as a fragment of geometric carpet, have been destroyed by a diagonal trench. The tesserae used for the panels are fine and well fitted, the density being around 150 tesserae per square decimeter. A variety of colored stones is represented, including white, gray, yellow, and black marble and colored limestone. Blue, yellow, red, and green glass paste and turquoise blue faience are also used in the figural motifs.[80] The eyes of the birds are made of small glass beads.

The subject of the mosaic makes it one of only a few known figural mosaics from Roman Alexandria.[81] Bird depictions in themselves are among the most popular themes in Egyptian mosaics. The bird panels from Kom al-Dikka echo representations of aquatic birds from the Hellenistic mosaic floors in Canopus and Thmuis.[82] While appearing deeply Egyptian in character at first glance, the decoration of this floor reveals artistic ties with other centers. For example, the orthogonal black-and-white pattern in the back of the room finds numerous parallels in mosaic floors from the western provinces of the Empire,[83] while the motif of two birds drinking from a cup is clearly borrowed from the Pergamon milieu.[84]

The arrangement of the decoration, particularly the geometric design in the back, indicates that the room may have served as a *cubiculum*. Like the other mosaic floors from the Villa of the Birds, it has been dated by the discoverer to the second century AD.[85]

Mosaic α-6

Only a small fragment of the border of this mosaic had been cleared in the course of the 1970–1971 excavations. Now it has been revealed in its entirety, following the removal of mosaic α-7 which had covered it. The tessellated floor has survived in relatively good condition, in two separate fragments (Fig. 30). The larger part on the south, measuring about 2 x 2 meters, includes a complete border and practically wholly preserved decorative panel (with the exception of some minor losses on the western and northern edges). The other part is much smaller and narrower (approximately 30 centimeters), and represents only part of the border. Originally, the floor had taken up all of the area of Room 6 (around 4.00 x 2.30 meters). The field decoration was asymmetrical in design, consisting of a polychrome central square irregularly contained within the surrounding bichrome geometric carpet.

Fig. 29: Mosaic α-6, fragment of a scroll and geometric border.

The carpet is edged on both sides by a single white filet, and additionally framed by a wide band of four rows of black tesserae.[86] The composition consists of a bichrome, orthogonal pattern of tangent, axially quartered circles, forming poised concave squares. The colors are counterchanged, creating the effect of a chessboard pattern.[87] The southern arm of the carpet is 1.72 meters long and 60 centimeters wide; the northern one, presumably much wider, must have originally been at least 1.60 meters wide, that is, it must have reached the northern wall of the room. This evident break with symmetry cannot be accidental; the idea was presumably to position the central panel opposite the doorway leading from the courtyard.

A band (5.5 centimeters wide)[88] of five rows of black tesserae separates the geometric carpet from the main square panel measuring 1.20 x 1.20 meters. The square is surrounded by a border decorated with inhabited acanthus scroll on a white ground. The full, practically circular scrolls of the ornament harmonize with the circles on the carpet (Fig. 29).

Fig. 30: Mosaic α-6, existing conditions record. (Drawing by G. Majcherek)

A single running scroll stems from an acanthus foot located in the center of the eastern side of the panel.[89] Inside each loop there are additional blue-red flower sprouts, pomegranates and *hederae* (stylized ivy leaf decorative elements), in the corner scrolls.[90] Flowers, sprouts, and pods are also used as space fillers. The vegetal ornament is made of tesserae in four principal colors: white for the background, mostly black and orange-red for the scrolling pattern, and turquoise-blue faience tesserae are used to decorate some tendrils, sprouts, and *hederae*.[91] The geometric carpet and the central panel are both made of tightly fit fine tesserae with a density of around 90–100 cubes per square decimeter.

The small-size *emblema*-type panel (51 x 51 centimeters) is framed with a black framing band of four rows of tesserae (5 centimeters wide). The corners of the panel are filled with small squares (5 x 5 centimeters). An almost square panel (Fig. 31) measuring 0.20 x 0.23 meters, framed by a crenelated border in the form of stepped triangles,[92] contains a representation of an animal in profile stepping to the right.

In the left part of the panel, behind the animal, there is a branch or tree. Despite the flawed body proportions, there can be little doubt that it is a panther. The bottom edge of the panel was repaired in antiquity, possibly obliterating the original iconographic arrangement. Two minor elements visible next to the paws of the panther seem to be the remains of the horns of another animal. Originally, the panther may have been attacking a gazelle, its paw already on the other animal's back. The representation of the panther, very often related to Dionysiac mythology, is not a very frequent theme on Egyptian mosaic floors.[93] The motif of a panther, tiger, or lion killing a gazelle or fawn is frequently employed in Roman mosaics with hunting scenes. It can be seen in mosaics from al-Djem[94] and mosaics from Isola Sacra in Ostia (unpublished).[95]

The *emblema* (decorative figural) type panel is executed of exceptionally fine cubes (approximately 0.3–0.6 centimeters in size, with a density of about 350 per square decimeter) and approaches *opus vermiculatum* (employing exceptionally fine cubes, with each side less than 5 millimeters, used most often for figural designs and emblemas) in quality.[96] The part with ancient repairs consists of slightly bigger and more irregular cubes.

Mosaic α–7

A bichrome tessellated mosaic with geometric pattern, this badly damaged and deteriorated mosaic was found superimposed over mosaic α–6. The single preserved fragment measured only 1.20 x 1.05 meters. The pattern consists of quartered squares surrounded by oblong tangent hexagons containing poised squares, outlined in double gray filet on a white background.[97]

The mosaic was made of rather large tesserae (1.5–2 centimeters) with a density approaching approximately 43–45 cubes per square decimeter, which is almost the same as mosaic α–2.

Chapter 2

Mosaics Conservation Work

Ewa Parandowska

Condition of the Mosaics

The full extent of the four mosaic floors was revealed in the course of the present conservation project. An assessment of the condition of particular mosaics carried out at the time their surfaces were cleared reveals some deterioration in their condition relative to what was recorded during the original excavations.

When excavated, the mosaics appeared to be in fairly good condition, although some fragments were almost completely lost: two panels with birds and a fragment of geometric design in mosaic α–5, and a major part of *opus sectile* pavement in α–3 and α–6. There was also further damage along the edges of all four mosaics, where the stone walls of the villa were dismantled (Fig. 43). Fragments featuring geometric decorations in mosaics α–2, α–3, and α–6 were quite well preserved. The bedding of these mosaics was stable in the major part and the tesserae were in good condition due to the hardness and low porosity of the stone of which they are made. In contrast, the mosaic α–3 and *opus sectile* pavement were in poor condition. In several places, a fire caused the breaking of tesserae and blackening of the surface (Fig. 21). In these zones, the bedding mortar lost its coherence and the tesserae could no longer adhere to the bedding. The stones and glass paste used for the bird panels in α–5 and the floral design in α–6 are very soft and porous. They have been seriously eroded by humidity and soluble salt migrations as well as by mechanical damage. The latter, induced by crumbling walls as well as by soil subsidence, caused serious deformation of the mosaic surfaces.

The eastern edges of pavements in α–2 and α–3 had settled about 20 centimeters below their original level. In α–3, along the western foundation wall, large cracks had formed and the tesserae at the edges of the cracks were detached (Fig. 32). In the mosaic α–6, beside the western edge, the settled area (approximately 50 square centimeters) had been severed from the rest of the mosaic. Due to the weakening of the bedding, the tesserae in this part of the mosaic had become loose and detached. Also the entire part of this mosaic which had been covered with a superimposed mosaic was found to be in a much worse condition than the rest of the floor. The tesserae were very dirty, their surface covered with traces of pink mortar. The bedding was weakened, the mortar had lost its cohesion, and tesserae had become detached.

The mosaics had been restored and protected in the past. There were two kinds of old repairs visible on the surface: ancient ones and modern ones from the 1970s.

In antiquity, the lacunae of the *opus sectile* mosaic α–3 were filled with colored marble slabs chosen at random, fixed rather carelessly with a dark mortar (Fig. 23). Small fragments of the guilloche in mosaic α–5 had been repaired in the same way. The *emblema* with the panther in α–6, arranged originally with very fine colored tesserae, was also reconstructed (Fig. 31). The repair was performed in similar stones but with slightly bigger tesserae, obliterating the original pattern (the goat-like animal has not been reconstructed).

In the 1970s, uncovered fragments of all four mosaics were temporarily protected, small lacunae were filled in, and edges were reinforced with cement mortar.

Fig. 31: Mosaics α-6, *emblema* with panther, showing previous reconstructions.

The Treatment

The policy adopted in this project aimed at in situ preservation of the mosaics and displaying the whole assemblage within its original architectural context.

Prior to conservation procedures two basic aims of preservation had been specified:

- Consolidation of mosaics in situ, preserving the irregularity of the surface and all ancient repairs. Removal of cement mortar used for protection in the 1970s.
- The reconstruction of small missing parts of pavements in the restoration effort. This was possible thanks to the retrieval of original materials and legible patterns. The reconstruction of small parts of the mosaics was suggested for technical and aesthetic reasons such as ease of perception.

The treatment consisted of:

- Temporary protection during excavations and unearthing of the mosaics.
- Long term preservation and conservation, which had to be individually adapted according to the condition of the different elements of the mosaics.

The conservation of the mosaics started on June 1, 1998, and was completed in three stages: the first from July 15 to August 8, 1998; the second from October 8 to December 12, 1998; and the third from February 1 to April 15, 1999.

Breaks in the conservation process were necessary in order to allow for the continuation of excavations along the eastern and southern wall of the shelter, to erect a roof over the mosaics (October–November 1998) and to build the niche for mosaic α–6 (January 1999).

Fig. 32: Mosaics α-2, α-3, and α-5 after temporary protection.

The working plan for the first stage consisted of the uncovering, documentation and restoration of mosaics α–2 and α–3. The second stage was devoted to the conservation of the multicolored mosaic with decorative panels (α–5). The third stage consisted of conservation and partial reconstruction of the *opus sectile* pavement (α–3) and full conservation treatment of mosaic α–6. The execution of the work was supervised by the author, and assisted by a local worker, Assam Mursi, trained in mosaic conservation.

Conservation Measures

Prior to undertaking the site work, it was essential to assess all theoretical and practical considerations bearing in mind the aims of conservation. It was also equally important to define areas of deterioration and estimate the extent of structural problems as well as the past history of repair. All aspects of the bedding structure, its composition and stratigraphy, were examined macroscopically under 4x magnification. The practical approach adopted consisted of the following measures:

- Unearthing and cleaning of the mosaic floors. All the mosaics were cleaned mechanically using brushes, scalpels, and blowers. Following reinforcement of the weakened parts of the mosaics, surfaces were washed carefully.
- Detailed documentation of the condition of mosaics (photographs, drawings, and recording of damage).
- Temporary protection of mosaic edges and borders of the lacunae. Edges of lacunae and borders of mosaics were temporarily reinforced with Japanese tissue paper and carboxymethylocellulose was chosen as glue. Paper facing was removed gradually during consolidation.
- Reinforcement of original bedding in weakened parts, and reinforcement of disintegrated tesserae. For consolidation and reinforcement of the original bedding, Primal E-330 and

Plextol B-500 (acrylic resin emulsions) 1:1 and 1:2 diluted in water were injected. In order to reduce surface tension, a solution of ethyl alcohol and water (1:1) was applied. Disintegrated tesserae were reinforced by impregnation with Paraloid B-72 in acetone and Paraloid B-82 in ethanol, both in a 20 percent solution.

- Removal of modern cement fillings and repairs. The cement mortar used in the 1970s for filling lacunae and protecting crumbling edges had to be removed mechanically with chisels and dentists' tools. The use of cement is unacceptable from a formal and aesthetic point of view, in light of recent research.
- Reconstruction (refilling of small lacunae) using original tesserae. The lacunae were recomposed with original tesserae found in the debris and with stone material similar to the original in shape and in color. Lime mortar with marble powder, and Primal emulsion was used as bedding (slaked lime, marble powder and Primal in the proportion 1:2:0.5).
- Protection of mosaic edges with lime mortar. Mortar composed of sand, lime and Plextol B-500, and acrylic resin emulsion was applied for protection of mosaic edges.
- Lifting and resetting the most damaged and distorted fragments, in their original position, on new fixed bedding.
- The edges of big lacunae along the wall foundations were protected by making permanent rims in lime mortar composed of washed coarse sand with a small (10 percent) addition of white cement. These large lacunae were then filled with loose gravel. The size and color of the gravel agrees with that of the original mosaics. The small lacunae (for example, in panels with birds) were filled with gray-colored mortar (lime mortar with marble powder in the proportion 1:3, with Plextol B-500 addition) to the level of the existing setting bed.

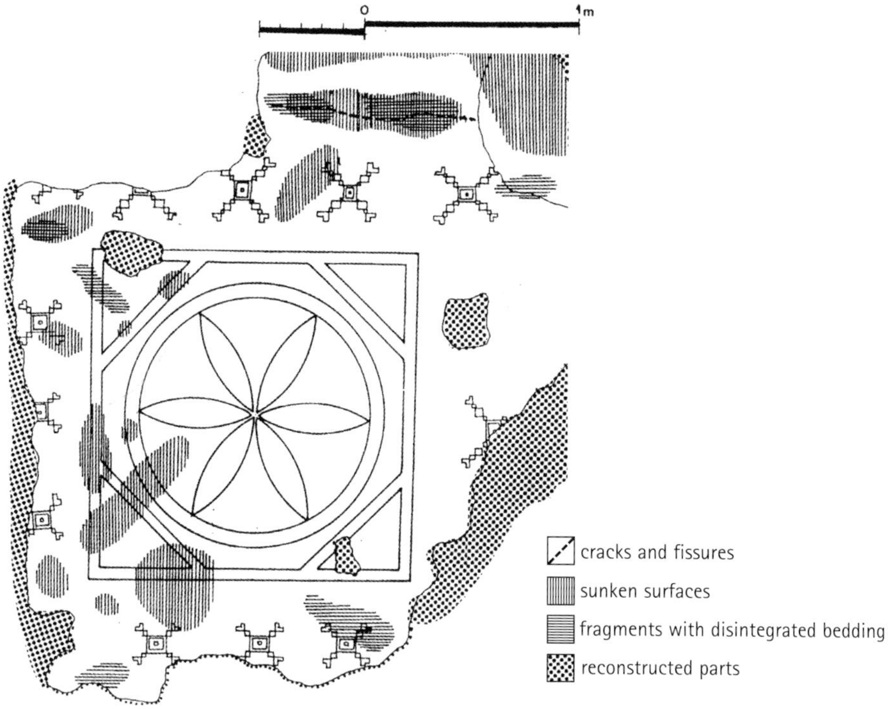

Fig. 33: Mosaic α-2, conservation record. (Drawing by E. Parandowska)

Fig. 34: Mosaic α-2, after conservation.

Conservation of Mosaic α-2 (Figs. 34 and 35)

About 15 percent of the original surface was missing. Some of the tesserae along the borders of the mosaic were lost; the surface was distorted and sagged. The bedding mortar was weakened and disintegrated. Small lacunae in geometric design were filled with cement in the 1970s.

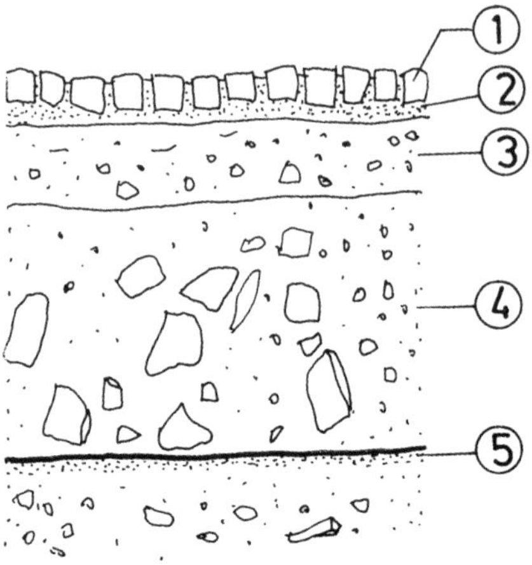

Fig. 35: Mosaic α-2, stratigraphical cross-section. (Drawing by G. Majcherek)

1. Tesserae, 1.5–2 cm thick;
2. Setting bed: layer of lime and marble powder some 0.5–1.0 cm thick;
3. Nucleus: layer of ground stones, ashes mixed with lime and sand, some 3–3.5 cm thick;
4. Rudus: concrete, some 12–15 cm thick;
5. Earlier floor.

The following conservation measures were taken:

- The surface was mechanically and chemically cleaned (rinsed and dried).
- Cement fillings of lacunae were removed mechanically.
- Lacunae were reintegrated and some parts of the mosaic edges were reconstructed with original tesserae found in the debris (Figs. 36 and 37).
- Some crumbled areas, edges, and cracks were stabilized with a soft mixture of mortar (lime, marble powder, and Plextol).

Fig. 36: Mosaic α-2, lacuna prepared for reconstruction.

Fig. 37: Mosaic α-2, lacuna after reconstruction.

Conservation of Mosaic α-3

Opus tesselatum floor (Fig. 38):

The physical condition of the two different parts of this pavement *(opus tesselatum* and *opus sectile)* varied considerably. Tesserae were in relatively good and stable condition because of the low porosity of the stone used prevented chemical damage.

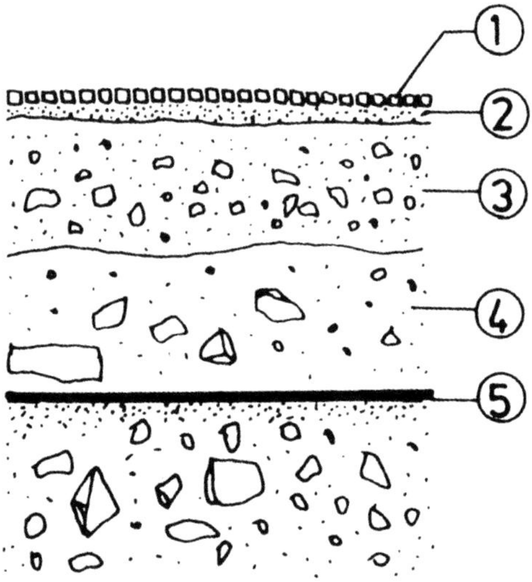

Fig. 38: Mosaic α-3, *opus tesselatum*, stratigraphical cross-section. (Drawing by G. Majcherek)

1. Tesserae (0.4–0.8 cm) made of basalt and white quartz;
2. Setting bed; layer of lime mortar ca. 0.5–1 cm thick;
3. Rudus; lime and coarse sand mortar, ca. 7 cm thick;
4. Clay mixed with rubble;
5. Earlier floor; lime mixed with crushed brick powder, surface painted red, ca. 1 cm thick.

There was much serious damage and loss of tesserae along the borders of the mosaic where the stone walls were plundered. Many black tesserae from the black strips that emphasized the mosaic edges were lost. In several sections a fire caused breakage of tesserae and darkening of the white background (Figs. 21 and 22). In those areas, the underlying mortar had lost its coherence and tesserae had come loose.

Severe cracking of bedding was observed. The mosaic was seriously distorted in its western part due to ground subsidence (Fig. 40). Consequently, a wide crack formed and the tesserae on the edge of the pavement were dislodged. In ancient repairs, big lacunae were filled with randomly set marble slabs (Fig. 42). Modern repairs from the 1970s were made using big tesserae and cement mortar (Fig. 43).

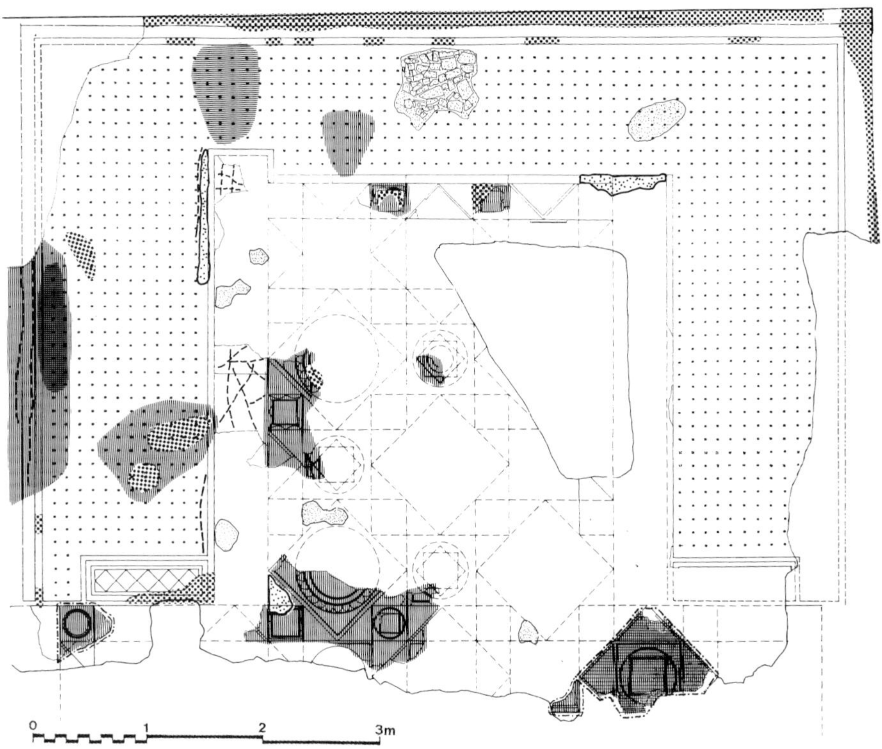

Fig. 39: Mosaic α-3, conservation record. (Drawing by E. Parandowska)

Fig. 40: Mosaic α-3, bedding cracking due to ground subsidence.

Fig. 41: Mosaic α-3, the same fragment during conservation.

Fig. 42: Northern part of mosaic α-3, with ancient repair.

Fig. 43: Mosaic α-3, modern repair of lacuna filled with cement and bigger tesserae.

The following conservation measures were taken:

- Consolidation of original bedding in the weakened parts with injections of Plextol emulsion diluted in water 1:2.
- Reestablishment of loose tesserae–two methods were chosen for this purpose. The direct method was applied to the small lacunae where lost tesserae were pressed into the soft lime mortar to fill the voids. In the other, indirect method, the tesserae were first reconstructed face down on canvas with the contour of the missing sections drawn in. The reconstructed section of the *tesselatum* mosaic was turned face up and put back in place in the bonding layer (lime, marble powder, acrylic resin). After checking and adjusting for adhesion, the cloth from the *tesselatum* surface was removed. Cracks and lacunae were filled using original tesserae or local materials similar to the original.

Fig. 44: Mosaic α-3, part of the *opus sectile* floor during conservation.

Opus sectile floor (Figs. 45, 46, and 47)

The *opus sectile* decoration was in a rather poor state, with only 15 percent of the original surface preserved. In antiquity, fire caused the weakening and disintegration of lime mortar used for arranging the decoration, and most of the colored tiles made of rare stones were plundered. The remaining fragments composed of thin marble tiles had also deteriorated due to surface erosion of soft material and other mechanical damages. The underlying mortar had lost its coherence and the tiles no longer adhered to the bedding. One of the aims of the conservation of this mosaic was to preserve all historical evidence; hence the decision was made to leave ancient repairs executed with big marble slabs chosen at random as well as all deformation and distortion of the surface. Modern repairs with the use of cement mortar had to be removed. Traces of the original pattern preserved in the bedding mortar were recorded (Fig. 45).

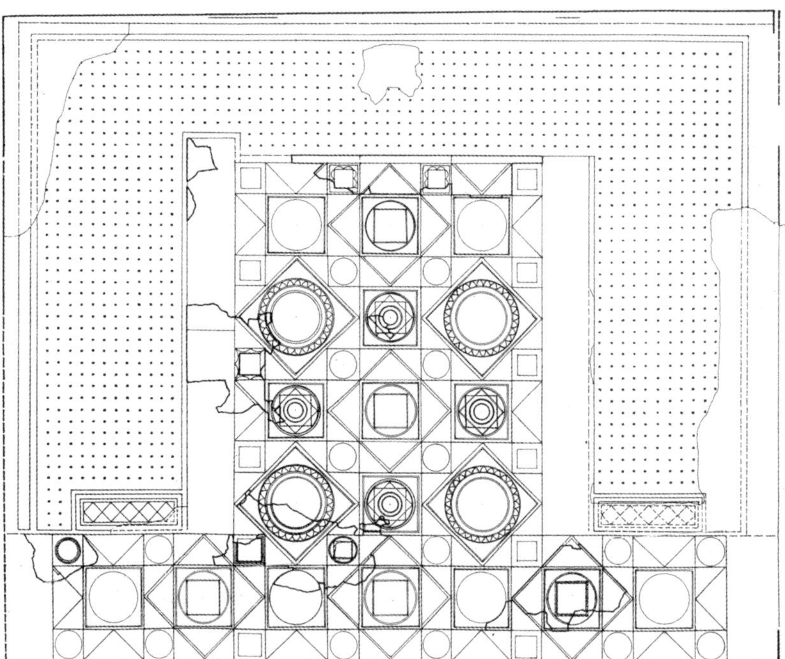

Fig. 45: Mosaic α-3, theoretical reconstruction. (Drawing by W. Kołątaj)

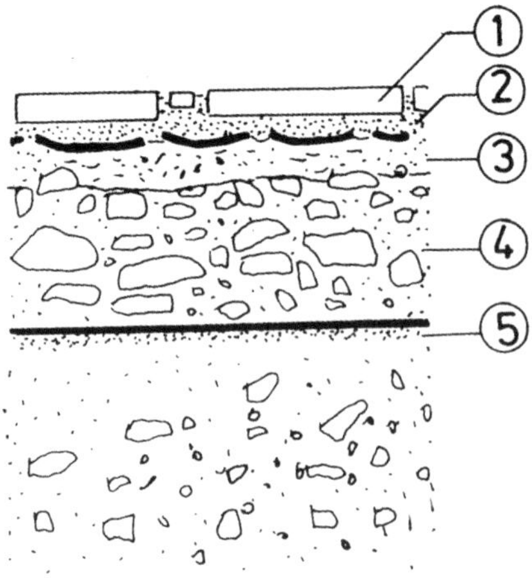

Fig. 46: Mosaic α-3, opus sectile part, stratigraphical cross-section. (Drawing by G. Majcherek)

1. Marble tiles of different thickness;
2. Setting bed: very thin (0.5 cm) layer of white lime mortar;
3. Rudus: lime and coarse sand mortar ca. 3.5 cm thick;
4. Statumen: stone rubble ca. 7 cm thick;
5. Earlier lime floor.

The following conservation measures were taken:

- Four fragments of decoration in *opus sectile* were traced (1:1) and detached from the bedding mortar. Remaining parts of decoration were lifted, then carefully cleaned and partially reconstructed (Fig. 44). A bedding of two layers of different mortars was applied to the reverse side of these fragments. First, a thin layer of lime, marble powder, and Plextol; and second, a lime, sand, and white cement mixture (in the proportion of 1:4:0.3) reinforced with stainless wire-netting. Fragments were fixed onto their original position.
- Other fragments of *opus sectile* decoration were provisionally protected with Japanese tissue paper facing, in order to prevent the fragile parts from further damage, then gradually reinforced with rich fluid mortar of lime and Plextol and left in situ (Fig. 47).

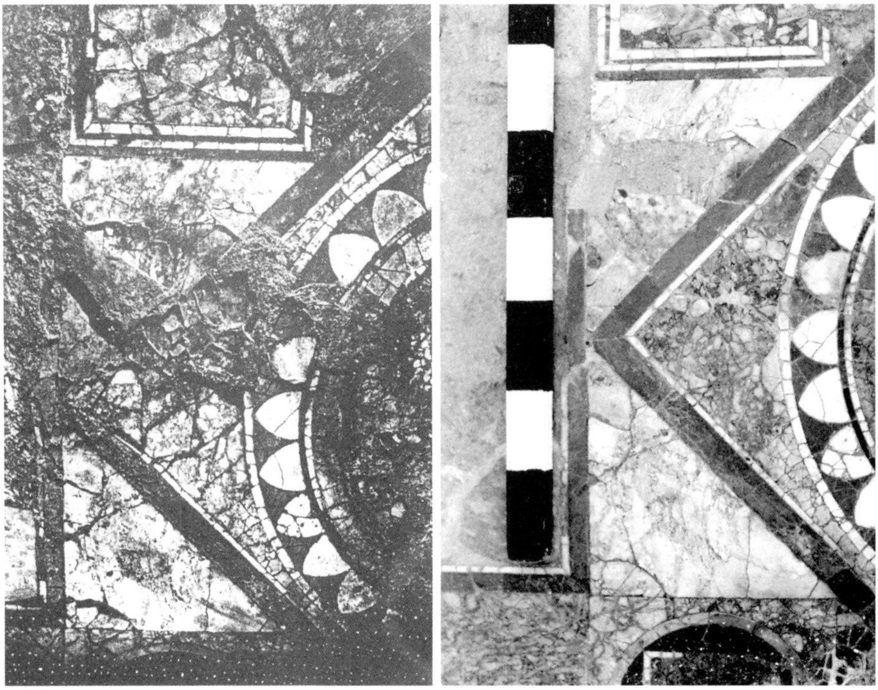

Fig. 47: Mosaic α-3, part of the opus sectile floor before and after conservation.

Conservation of Mosaic α-5

About 30 percent of the surface of this mosaic had been lost completely (Figs. 48 and 51). Two of the panels with birds, large fragments of the geometric design, and decoration along the edges of the mosaic were missing. The underlying soil had sagged and shifted and the surface was distorted due to mechanical damages, namely, collapsed roof and walls. The glass tesserae were very soft and had disintegrated or were seriously eroded by soluble salt activity due to the high alkaline content of the glass paste. In many parts where the glass paste was used for decoration, only remnants of the colors and shape of tesserae could be seen. In ancient times, a fire caused darkening of the mosaic surface and disintegration of the bedding mortar in several places (Figs. 26 and 27). In antiquity, small lacunae had been filled with white marble pieces.

Fig. 48: Mosaic α-5, conservation record. (Drawing by E. Parandowska)

Fig. 49: Mosaics α-2 and α-5, before conservation.

Fig. 50: Mosaic α-5, panels with birds before and after conservation.

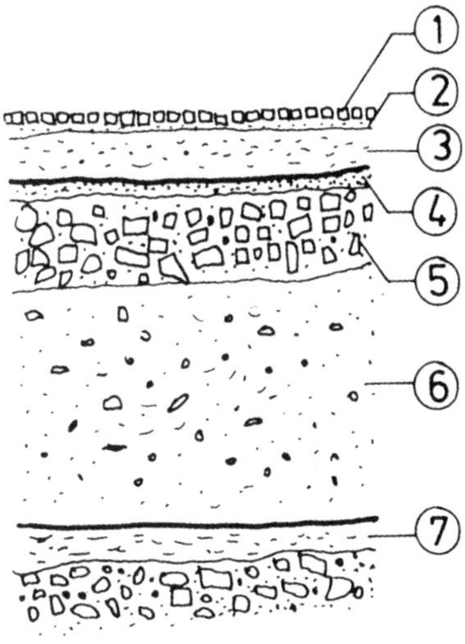

Fig. 51: Mosaic α-5, stratigraphical cross-section. (Drawing by G. Majcherek)

1. Tesserae: multicolored made of marble, soft stones, and glass paste;
2. Setting bed: layer of lime and marble powder, ca. 0.5–0.7 cm thick;
3. Nucleus: layer of lime mixed with sand, ashes and charcoal, ca. 2–3 cm thick;
4. Earlier floor;
5. Statumen: stone blocks, ca. 5–6 cm thick;
6. Leveling layer;
7. Earlier floor.

The following conservation measures were taken:

- Detailed photographs and 1:1 tracings of all lacunae and sensitive zones were made.
- The surface was cleaned mechanically (with brushes) and chemically (with water and sponges).
- Edges were provisionally protected with Japanese tissue paper.
- Modern repairs with cement were removed mechanically using chisels and dentists' tools. A protective band of cement applied on mosaic edges was replaced with lime mortar.
- The weak tesserae, small in size that had eroded, mainly those made in glass or very soft stones, were treated individually with Paraloid B-60 diluted in ethanol.
- Some fragments of decoration were reconstructed. Reconstruction was done in the small lacunae, on the mosaic edges and in parts of the panels where there was no doubt as to the shape and color of the design. The reconstruction was possible thanks to the preserved colored ground and retrieval of original material (glass paste and tesserae), found during excavations in the debris. In some places, the setting bed still retained the imprint of the tesserae with preserved traces of the original stones and glass paste attached to the ground. The resetting of tesserae and reconstruction of disintegrated fragments were carried out with the help of a 2.5x magnifying glass.
- After reconstruction of the wall foundations, missing parts of the mosaic bedding and big lacunae were filled with new mortar and gravel.

Fig. 52: Mosaic α-5, panel with duck before and after conservation.

Fig. 53: Mosaic α-5, panel with parrot before and after conservation.

Fig. 54: Mosaic α-5, panel with peacock before and after conservation.

Fig. 55: Mosaic α-5, panel with pigeon before and after conservation.

Fig. 56: Mosaic α-5, panel with two pigeons before and after conservation.

Fig. 57: Mosaic α-5, panel with quail before and after conservation.

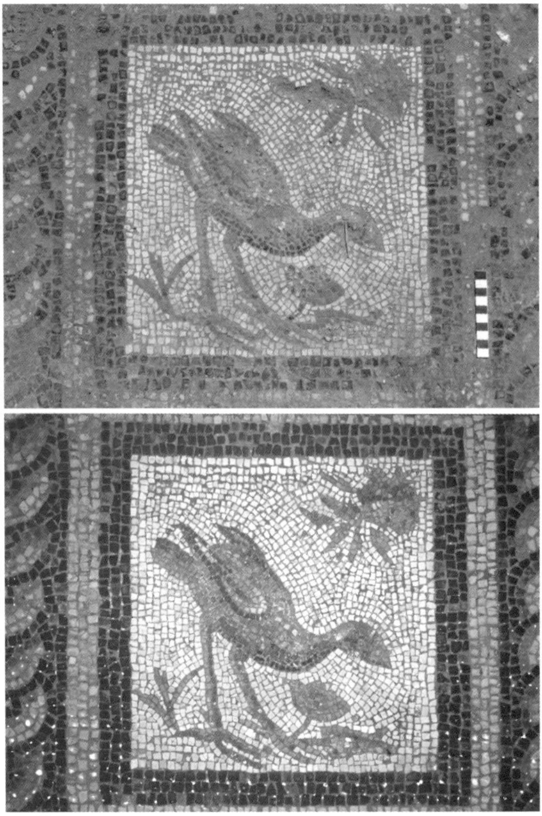

Fig. 58: Mosaic α-5, panel with purple gallinule before and after conservation.

Conservation of Mosaic α-6

About 20 percent of the original surface was missing (Fig. 30). The mosaic was preserved in two separated fragments. A long diagonal gap, about 50 centimeters wide, separates the northern part of the geometric decoration from the rest of the pavement. Tesserae along the edges of the mosaic were loose. The central part of the pavement had been covered in antiquity with a fragment of the superimposed geometric mosaic α–7. Remnants of this mosaic were lifted and transferred to the store. The remains of the pink bedding mortar of the lifted fragment covered the surface of the central part of the mosaic. In this part, the bedding had disintegrated and tesserae were crumbling. The blue faience tesserae had eroded, and their surface was very dark and deteriorated. The western

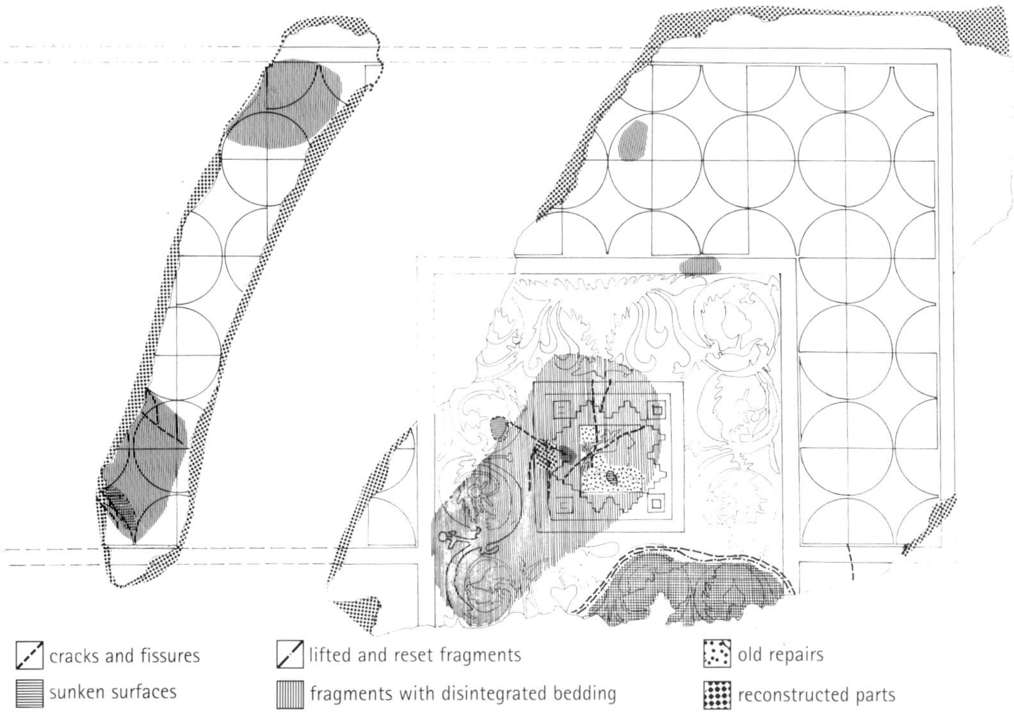

Fig. 59: Mosaic α-6, conservation record. (Drawing by E. Parandowska)

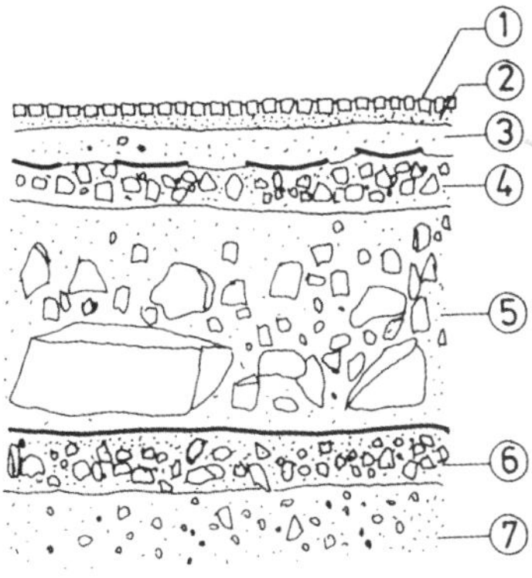

Fig. 60: Mosaic α-6. Stratigraphical section. (Drawing by G. Majcherek)

1. Tesserae (1–1.5 cm);
2. Setting bed: a white layer of lime and marble powder (0.5–1 cm thick);
3. Nucleus: layer of dark-gray lime mortar mixed with ashes (1.5–2.5 cm);
4. Rudus: coarse lime mortar mixed with ground stones and crushed pottery shards;
5. Statumen: concrete of grind stones and smashed pieces of old plaster mixed with soil, about 5 cm thick;
6. Earlier floor prepared with lime mortar painted red about 2 cm thick;
7. Preparatory bedding of ground limestone 15–20 cm thick, mixed with soil.

half of *emblema* with the representation of a panther was reconstructed with slightly bigger tesserae (3–5 millimeters), obliterating the original design (Fig. 31). Several distortions, both small and large, were observed on the surface. A fragment of mosaic about 50 square centimeters in size with vegetal decoration beside the western edge had sagged and shifted about 10 centimeters lower. The sunken mosaic in this part was seriously disintegrated, tesserae dislodged and crumbling (Fig. 62).

The following conservation measures were taken (Fig. 59):

- Temporary protection of the edges of the mosaic and all weakened parts with Japanese tissue paper and carbomethylocellulose.
- Reinforcement of disintegrated and crumbling tesserae; injections and impregnation with Paraloid B-60.
- Resetting of disintegrated fragments; injections with Plextol B-500 and Primal E-330 and a soft mixture of lime, marble powder, and Primal in proportions of 1:2:0.5.
- Partial reconstruction of all small lacunae and weakened edges.
- Lifting of the disintegrated fragment. Due to the sunken bedding, deformation of the surface and disintegration of the cubes, the fragment measuring approximately 50 square centimeters had to be lifted and replaced in situ on a new fixed bedding. The fragment was carefully cleaned and the soil from the edges cleared away. Loose tesserae were collected, bagged, and their location marked on a 1:1 tracing (Fig. 61). The cut lines were traced on a 1:1 drawing. The edges of cut lines on the mosaic were protected with Japanese tissue facing.
- Facing of the fragment with gauze tissue and a second layer of canvas using carboxymethylocelullose as glue. The faced fragment had to be dried with hot air, using a hair dryer. The fragment was removed and its reverse cleaned mechanically. The new bedding was prepared using lime and sand mortar with 0.5 percent of white cement to reset the lifted fragment, while lime, marble powder, and Plexol were used to make a bonding layer.

Fig. 61: Fragment of mosaic α-6, condition documentation by tracing prior to lifting of the mosaic section.

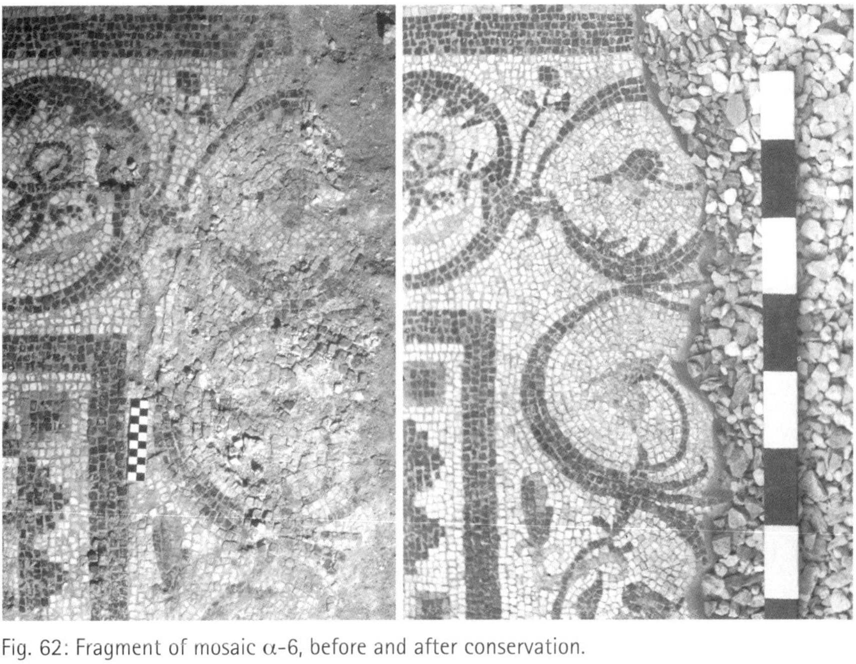

Fig. 62: Fragment of mosaic α-6, before and after conservation.

- Cleaning involved the removal of all calcareous accretion and remnants of superimposed bedding mortar from the surface of the mosaic, mechanically, with scalpels and fiberglass brushes.
- Reinforcement of the edges of the mosaic. Preserved fragments of this mosaic were uncovered down to the earlier floor level (approximately 25 centimeters deeper), then overlaid with lime and sand mortar, with a small addition of white cement.

Conservation of Mosaic α-7

It was decided to lift and transfer the mosaic onto the new bedding since its position interfered with the planned construction of the eastern end of the southern retaining wall. Due to the limited dimensions of the excavation trench, the mosaic was divided into three smaller, more manageable pieces.

Cloth facing was then fixed using polyvinilum acetate as glue. After drying, cutting lines were carefully marked on the textile, and sections

Fig. 63: Mosaic α-7, during cleaning.

of the mosaics were detached from their original bedding. Subsequently, remains of the old bedding adhering to the reverse of the tesserae were removed.

New bedding (approximately 3 centimeters thick) was made of lime and cement mortar reinforced with stainless wire-netting. Separate fragments were merged using additional wire-netting and a layer of mortar.

The mosaic is displayed in Room 6, as a separate panel placed approximately 15 centimeters over the missing fragment of the mosaic α–6.

Aeration and Drainage

The mosaics were preserved in situ, on their original beddings. Since large lacunae were not filled, nor were deformed mosaic surfaces rectified, it seemed advisable, for conservation reasons, to introduce aeration pipes around the preserved fragments.

Perforated plastic flexible pipe F 4 (3.8 centimeters) was installed about 20 centimeters below the level of the mosaics, embedded in a loosely strewn gravel backfill, to assure aeration of the bedding and to ease the evaporation of humidity. This measure will certainly protect the mosaics against micro-organisms developing in the bedding, and will also accelerate the drying of moisture that still remains in the soil. Possible salt crystallization will thus be limited to the immediate vicinity of the pipes.

Chapter 3

Archaeological and Functional Assumptions

Wojciech Kołątaj

Shelter Design and Construction

The conservation of the mosaic floors was a very urgent issue. Their location in the lowest point of the excavation area made them especially sensitive to damage caused by repeated rainfall flooding. Seeping water is dangerous to the stability and soundness of the floor substructure, leading to quick disintegration. Consequently, any conservation work required not only direct conservation treatment of the ancient floors, but also the erection of a shelter, an appropriate restructuring of the immediate surroundings, and the establishment of an efficient water drainage system.

In view of the general development of the site, the Supreme Council of Antiquities (SCA) decided to include the domestic quarter in the planned tourist zone, and especially to display the set of unique Early Roman mosaic floors. SCA's plans for an archaeological park to be established on the site of Kom al-Dikka were instrumental in helping to overcome all kinds of difficulties and obstacles usually accompanying the conservation of objects left in place (Figs. 3 and 65). Issues such as access to the mosaic floor exhibition, placing the display in the surrounding context, and future maintenance were resolved from the start with proper landscaping, the arrangement of tourist paths, and preparation of a guard room. Furthermore, in situ conservation is in accordance with currently preferred exhibition principles and the International Committee for the Conservation of Mosaics recommendations.

Two factors played a major role in the shelter design: its protecting role and the form of the surrounding remains of ancient architecture. The site of the uncovered mosaic floors determines the character of the shelter as part of the ancient architectural exhibition at Kom al-Dikka. The mosaic floors are located in the southeastern end of the site (Fig. 3). This part of the excavations, east of street R4, constitutes the fragment of an insula wholly taken up by domestic architecture (Fig. 64). The relics of Early Roman and Late Roman/Byzantine architecture, small in size and surviving in rather poor condition, differ substantially from the nearby public structures, especially the nearest and best-preserved cistern complex. The planned tourist route will lead tourists naturally from the theater to the cisterns along the confines of the excavation area, and down some steps to the level of street R4, from where the roof of the shelter and its glass west wall opening on a green patio will enclose the view to the east, above the walls of the reconstructed Late Roman/Byzantine domestic architectural complex (Fig. 65). The newly built northern gate of the site will most probably be used as an exit only.

The shelter's design was determined by its principal function, namely, the protection of the ancient mosaic floors. To preserve harmony with the surrounding ruins, the shelter could not be too bold in color or shape. Furthermore, the costs of execution had to be reasonable. The topography of the area, where the shelter was to be erected, made it necessary to take into consideration not only the conformity of directions of particular spatial elements, but also the difficult design problem of linking the shelter roof with the 8 meter high and steeply sloping (40-degree inclination) escarpment rising immediately next to the projected building on the south and east (Fig. 2). The large gabled

Fig. 64: Shelter among the Byzantine architecture east of R4 street.

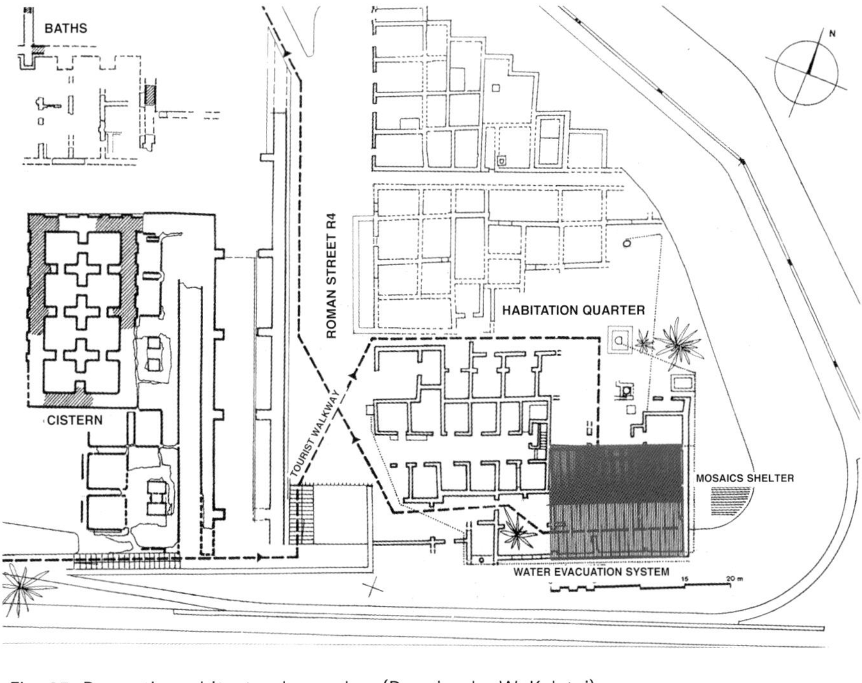

Fig. 65: Domestic architectural complex. (Drawing by W. Kołątaj)

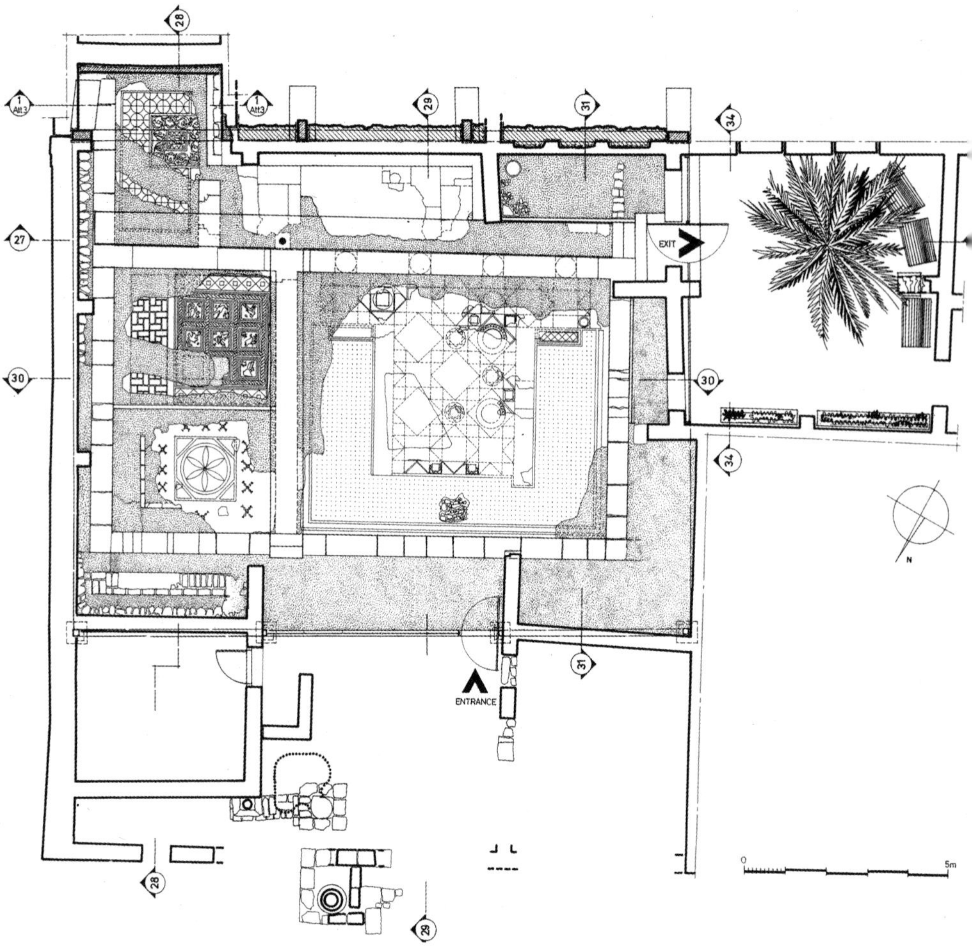

Fig. 66: Shelter ground floor plan. (Drawing by W. Kołątaj)

surface of the shelter roof (180 square meters), when viewed from above, that is, from Safiya Zaghloul Street, would be seen surrounded by a complex of previously restored Late Roman/Byzantine architecture. Neither its color nor form could conflict with this architecture.

The suggested design was a gable roof similar to ancient examples in its slope and proportions. Instead of using roof tiles, as was done in antiquity, corrugated steel sheets were provided. A beige color was chosen as closest to the natural patina of the surrounding ruins. Sheets of corrugated plate below the eaves also concealed the head of the trusses with a 70-centimeter band.

Nowhere does the roof come in direct contact with the surrounding ancient walls; it is separated either by the structural supporting beams or by glass. The idea was to divide the roof clearly and simplify it to the maximum extent, as well as to avoid having it appear to dominate the ancient substance. This condition was met by inserting glass in the gables of the roof, with the divisions repeating the arrangement of the glass windows below. The side edges of the roof are covered by wooden planks, painted beige, screening the thickness of the roofing. The roof surface passes directly into the upper parts of the walls from the north and south, whereas the gables from the west and east are closed with glass panels. The 130 centimeter rise of the roof is correlated with the walls of the surrounding Late Roman/Byzantine buildings. Gutters mounted along the northern and southern edges emphasize the simplicity of its form.

The exposed trussed structure of the roof, with a span of twelve meters, is supported only by outer beams that are hidden from internal view. The whole structure of the roof has been painted white to reflect light. The Styrofoam sheets are also white. Thus, the structure of the roof does not distract the attention of viewers.

The entrance is from the north side, set in a glass wall joining two symmetric parts of Late Roman/Byzantine buildings (Fig. 68). The mosaic floors of the Early Roman villa, which are the object of exhibition here, are situated about 1.5 meters below the entrance level.

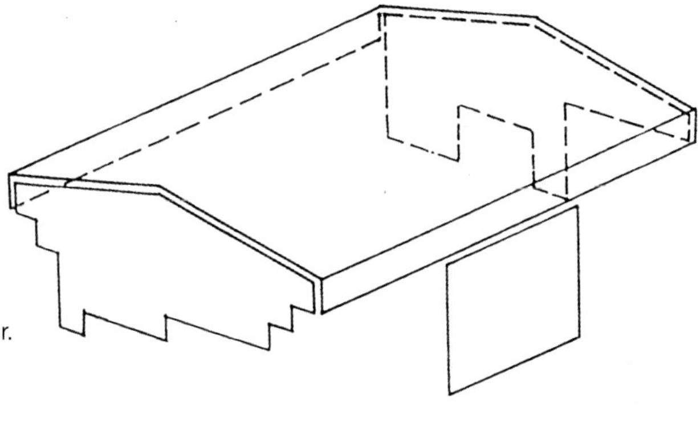

Fig. 67. The design of the shelter. (Drawing by W. Kołątaj)

The entrance platform is big enough for a group of about a dozen visitors (Fig. 68). Extending from it is an 80-centimeter-wide walkway, suspended a meter above the mosaic floors and permitting a view of the whole exhibition. Visitors follow the walkway, view the mosaics, and move toward the exit, where there is an area for resting in the shade.

Early Roman Villa *Alpha*—Conservation Procedures

The elements of ancient architecture on display are presented on two separate levels. The remains of the villa—the ancient walls and restored parts of the structure, as well as mosaic floors—are all located below the

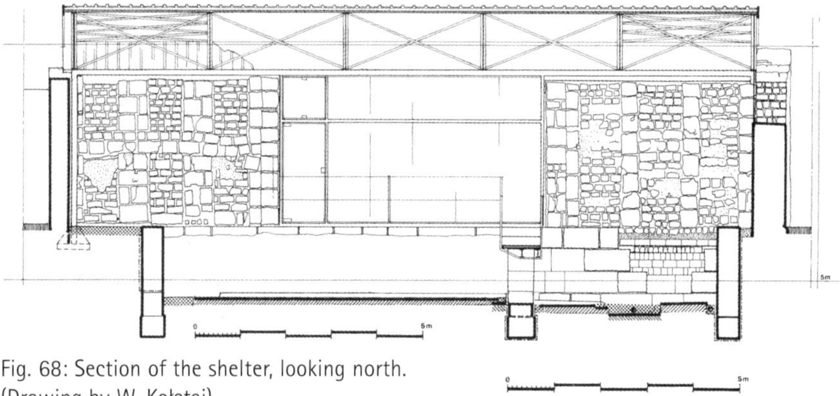

Fig. 68: Section of the shelter, looking north.
(Drawing by W. Kołątaj)

Fig. 69: East elevation, concept design superimposed over a photograph of the site.
(Drawing by W. Kołątaj)

Fig. 70: West elevation. (Drawing by W. Kołątaj)

level of the entrance. The Late Roman/Byzantine walls, located at a higher level and built using a different technique, now serve as part of the shelter walls. Where the ancient walls were missing, glass panels were installed. The shelter is thus a kind of glass box inserted among Late Roman/Byzantine walls, the irregular forms of which form the backdrop for the display.[98]

In accordance with the architectural conception of the shelter, some sections of the Late Roman/Byzantine walls restored in the 1970s had to be removed, as their course interfered with the mosaic exhibition. Partition walls of Rooms B1–B3 were consequently dismantled, along with the annexes in the courtyard (b1–b3), after having been recorded in sufficient detail. The eastern elevation of Rooms F3 and F4 was also removed, as were the partition walls in F1, F2, and F3 (Figs. 6 and 87).

Other outer walls of the Late Roman/Byzantine buildings were treated in a diametrically different way. The exceptionally thick eastern wall of House B (approximately 65 centimeters), reconstructed in the upper part, was used as an outer wall for the shelter. The southern and the western walls of House F, shared with House D, were also used as shelter walls.

Fig. 71: Early Roman and Byzantine walls after reconstruction, looking east.

Fig. 72: Southern wall of the Byzantine Room B1 before removal.

They ensure the proper harmonization of the new construction with the existing ancient remains. Room B4, which was adapted to serve as a temporary conservation workshop, was left unchanged and will be used in the future for a local guard (Figs. 75 and 76).

The mutual relation of the villa walls and the Late Roman/Byzantine structure above is entirely accidental. Furthermore, the shelter only protects the northeastern part of the villa, since the rest of it is still buried under the escarpment to the south, which could not be removed for reasons of safety (Fig. 14). The courtyard, usually the focal organization unit of ancient houses, has been uncovered here only in a small part. Thus, the southern confines of the area are formed by the walls of Late Roman/Byzantine structures, which were thickened and reinforced with concrete pillars and beams, as required, thus serving simultaneously as a revetment wall for the escarpment (Figs. 66 and 76). The construction of a retaining wall with damp-proofing on the south side of the area necessitated the removal of some previously uncovered fragments of geometrical mosaic floor α–7. The removal of mosaic floor α–7 revealed a central panel with color and figural motifs belonging to mosaic α–6 immediately below. This discovery prompted a change in the shelter design in order to display the entire Room α–6. The south wall of Room B1 of the Late Roman/Byzantine building was taken down and a niche measuring 3.5 x 1.7 meters was constructed in the southern shelter wall (Figs. 66 and 75). This required further earthworks (a deep trench dug into the southern escarpment), building works (reinforced concrete walls and roof of the niche), and conservation works (conservation of mosaic α–6 and placing of mosaic α–7 on a new bedding), obviously extending the scope of the original project. The niche, which is not visible from the outside, has not disturbed the external integrity of the design. From the inside, thc niche appears on the eastern extreme of the southern wall, dividing it visually into two parts.

Both the upper part of the niche and the socle of the Late Roman/Byzantine wall on the earth fill were cased in concrete walls

(Fig. 73). Their function as escarpment casing walls is apparent by their form and texture.

The excavated remains of the villa form a fragment of the larger residential quarter dated to the first to second century AD. Recent excavations have clarified the relations between particular buildings. Other, similar buildings have been found to adjoin the villa in question on the north and east. Testifying to this are remains of other mosaic floors found nearby, at higher levels (1.20 meters).

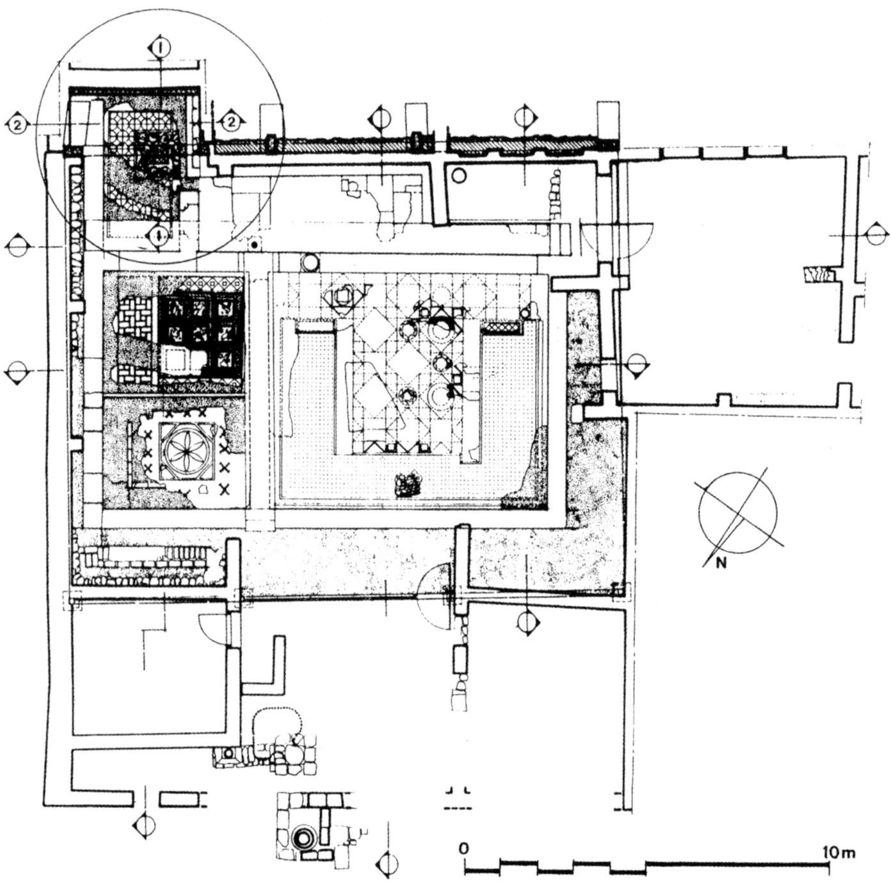

Fig. 73: Niche situation within the shelter. (Drawing by W. Kołątaj)

A partly surviving fragment of a wall belonging to the adjacent villa, and general dimensions of a building lot, permitted the theoretical reconstruction and anastylosis of the outer walls. Archaeological excavations revealed that the internal walls of the villa had been almost entirely removed in the past. There are only a few places where large blocks of the original walls structured in isodomic technique (measuring about 50 x 50 x 100 centimeters) survive above the floor level. Thanks to additional evidence yielded by fragmentarily preserved foundations made of small stones bonded in clay mortar, it was possible to trace the course of the walls with considerable accuracy. Large limestone blocks found in the debris were used for anastylosis.

The significant difference of levels between the floors and the foundations of the Late Roman/Byzantine structures above required either the missing Early Roman walls to be reconstructed to the height of 3–4 courses (1.5–2 meters), or else entirely new casing walls to be erected (Fig. 74). Both methods were used depending on local conditions. The outer wall, enclosing Rooms 2, 5, and 6 from the east, was rebuilt using new limestone blocks (sizes and bonding identical to the original ones known from other buildings excavated at the site) as well as blocks found in the debris (Figs. 75 and 76). The northern outer wall of the Room 2 was reconstructed only to a low level, to enable a view over the original part of the outer wall of the neighboring villa. It turned out that the northern wall of the *triclinium* had been wrongly restored in the 1970s as a structure built of small irregular blocks in order to secure the edges of the then newly discovered mosaic. To avoid misinterpretation, it was now decided to apply a new plaster coating supplemented with small fragments of original plaster found in the debris. As it was impossible to extend the excavation to the west, it could not be determined whether there were other rooms abutting the courtyard and *triclinium* on this side. In view of this, the western wall of the *triclinium* was partly reconstructed only in places where it was certain that there were no doorways.

Architectural research and precise recording permitted the theoretical reconstruction of the *triclinium* floor with its complicated design, which constitutes a combination of an *opus tesselatum* frame and *opus sectile* center field. Only 15 percent of the original surface of the *opus sectile* field survived. Imprints of an original composition made of squares, triangles, and circles were found clearly preserved in the bedding (Fig. 23). The well-preserved bedding structure reveals an ancient paving technique. Moreover, precision of the floor design based on Roman feet (approximately 29.7 centimeters) also allows for the hypothetical reconstruction of the position of columns separating the *triclinium* from the courtyard (Fig. 12). A fragment of limestone cornice unearthed in the uncovered part of the courtyard allows reconstruction of the whole architectural order (Fig. 13). In all the rooms, remnants of earlier floors were recorded. They were identified both chronologically and technologically.

The exhibition of Early Roman villa mosaic floors in the shelter, together with parts of reconstructed walls and some architectural decoration elements found there, also displays consecutive levels of habitation and differences in the nature of each.

Exiting the shelter, the visitors can either turn toward the entrance gate or else continue the visit in a westerly direction along the baths and toward the Theater Portico.

The situation of the pavilion on the southern tourist walkway just by the entrance from Safiya Zaghloul Street secures its proper exposition and enriches this part of the excavation area. The differences in ancient architecture on either side of Street R4 are thus emphasized. The towering structure of the cistern, vast red-brick ruins of the baths, lofty columns of the gymnasium, entrance gate and staircase are balanced not only in their urbanistic context but also technically.

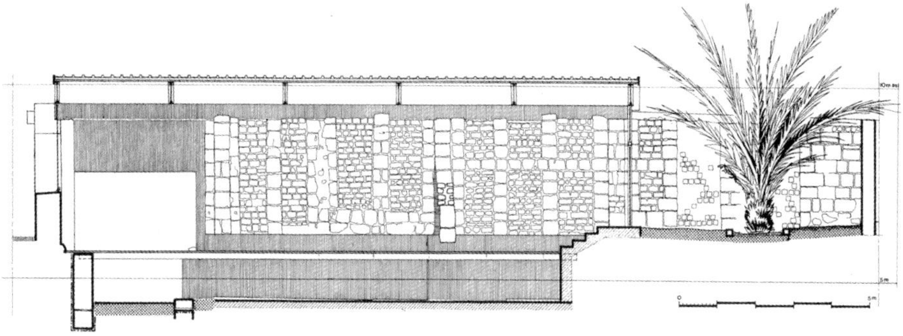

Fig. 74. Section of the shelter, looking south; cf. Fig. 66. (Drawing by W. Kołątaj)

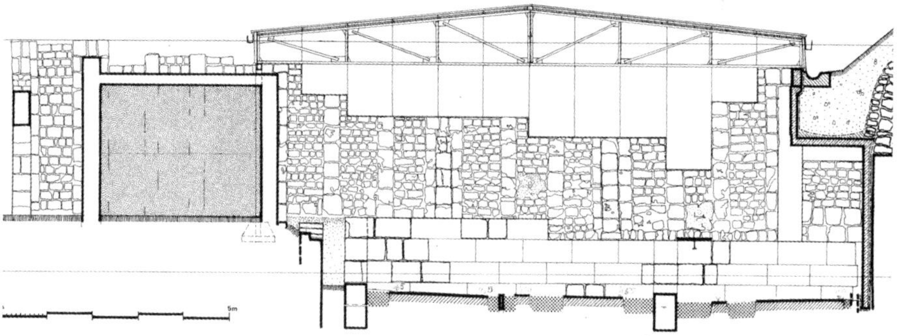

Fig. 75. Section of the shelter, looking east, showing the niche with the Panther Mosaic α-6; cf. Fig. 66. (Drawing by W. Kołątaj)

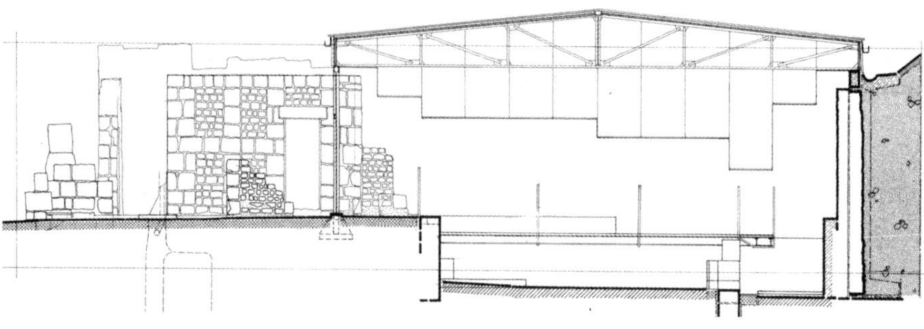

Fig. 76. Section of the shelter; cf. Fig. 66. (Drawing by W. Kołątaj)

Chip Vincent

Eastern part of the Kom al-Dikka site with the shelter erected over the Villa of the Birds.

Chip Vincent

Mosaics within the shelter, view looking southwest. The Rosette Mosaic α-2 is in the foreground, the Birds Mosaic α-5 in the center, and the niche with the Panther Mosaic α-6 in the back.

Chip Vincent

Mosaics within the shelter, view looking northwest over the Birds Mosaic α-5 and the Rosette Mosaic α-2. In the back, visible through a gap in the masonry, is a wall of a neighboring early Roman house, and above it, late Roman walls incorporated into the structure of the shelter.

Chip Vincent

Mosaics within the shelter, view looking northeast over the *triclinium* floor α-3, with its central part of *opus sectile* surrounded on three sides with *opus tesselatum*.

Edwin C. Brock

The Rosette Mosaic α-2. North is at the top of the picture.

Edwin C. Brock

The Birds Mosaic α-5. North is at the top of the picture.

Chip Vincent (1); Tara Todras-Whitehill (5)

Images of birds on the side and corner panels of the Birds Mosaic α-5. Upper row: parrot, purple gallinule, quail (or partridge); lower row: peacock, teal, pigeon.

Tara Todras-Whitehill

Central panel of the Birds Mosaic α-5 with two pigeons drinking from a cup.

Chip Vincent

Conservator Ewa Parandowska at work on the Birds Mosaic α-5, conserved in situ.

Chip Vincent

The Panther Mosaic α-6. North is to the left of the picture.

Chip Vincent

Central panel of the Panther Mosaic α-6. Ancient alterations to the mosaic are visible.

Tara Todras-Whitehill

Fragment of geometric mosaic α-7 mounted on a new bedding.

Tara Todras-Whitehill

Mosaic floor of the *triclinium* (α-3), view looking northwest. In the background, partially restored walls of the Villa of the Birds, and late Roman structures above them.

Edwin C. Brock

Fragment of the *opus sectile* floor of the *triclinium* (α-3.)

Edwin C. Brock

Southeastern corner of the *triclinium* (mosaic floor α-3). Fragments of *opus sectile* (front) and *opus tesselatum* (back). Bedding with a pattern laid out with pieces of amphorae is clearly visible.

Chapter 4

The Shelter Design

Wojciech Kołątaj

The shelter, measuring 15 x 12 meters, was designed to protect the mosaics from the detrimental effects of atmospheric factors, mainly rainwater. The protection of mosaic floors from direct sunshine also reduces the danger of daily thermal expansion, and last but not least, it protects against destruction caused by visitors.

Fig. 77: Wooden form for southern concrete beam.

Structural requirements as well as the specification of the steel sections and roof tiling available on the local market led to the adoption of a basic 3 x 3 meter structural module. Such a module ensures the almost perfect adjustment of the shelter to the existing remains of ancient architecture (Fig. 66). The roof-supporting structure of the shelter is structurally independent from the ancient walls. Girders of the gabled roof rest from the north on four pillars and a steel beam (Figs. 79 and 80), and from the south, on four pillars and a reinforced concrete beam. This differentiation is the result of having to combine two different functions inside a single architectural unit: a roof-supporting structure, and reinforcement of the revetment wall supporting the adjacent escarpment (Fig. 78).

The height of the shelter between the level of the mosaics and the ceiling amounts to 5.5 meters. The mosaics are, however, situated 1.5 meters lower than the ground level and the level of the footbridge. There are no internal supports to conflict aesthetically in any way with the extant ancient ruins. As mentioned previously, the shelter's outer wall

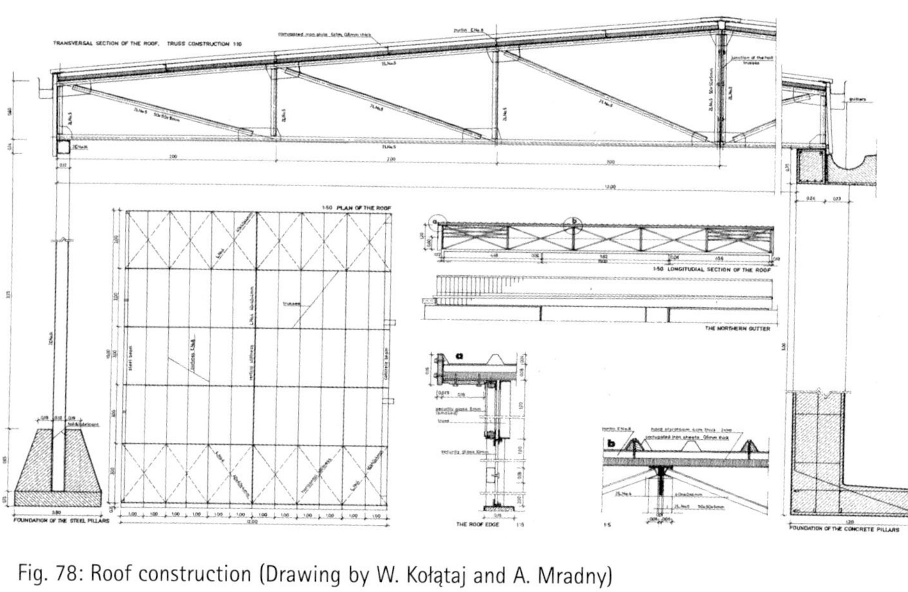

Fig. 78: Roof construction (Drawing by W. Kołątaj and A. Mradny)

was designed to adjust to the existing walls of the Late Roman/Byzantine buildings. Their preserved height determines the minimum possible height of the shelter. In places where Late Roman/Byzantine walls did not survive or were preserved in lower courses only, new walls made of security glass panels were introduced.

The southern part of the roof-supporting structure consists of a reinforced concrete beam, placed on four reinforced concrete pillars measuring 26 x 50 centimeters by 5.5 meters tall. These pillars simultaneously form an important element of the revetment wall. Both outer pillars were set with their longer sides attached to the Late Roman/Byzantine walls. Intermediate pillars were built perpendicular to the said wall in order to counteract the pressure of the escarpment (Figs. 66 and 78).

Fig. 79: Southern beam reinforcement during assembly.

Reinforced footings of the pillars were shaped as platforms some 30–40 centimeters thick, measuring 1.20 x 0.60 meters. This type of construction protects the whole structure against tilting caused by the escarpment. The footing reaches some 40–50 centimeters below the level of mosaics. The retaining wall, widening an existing Late Roman/Byzantine wall from the south, was built of limestone blocks joined with lime and cement mortar (in proportions of 1:2:5). Both structures were separated and insulated with two-layered polystyrene foil.

The southern concrete beam measuring 26 x 35 centimeters was reinforced in tensile working cross-sections with steel fabric Q_R 3600 kg/cm^2 2 x f 20 + 2 x f 16, and in other non loading sections: 2 x f 16. Shackles (f 6) set every 25 centimeters were used.

The northern beam was made of channel bars 2x [140 welded to the top of steel pillars (Fig. 81). Outer pillars were made of welded channel bars 2x [140; middle pillars (1 x [140) were additionally filled with concrete. Foundations of the rigidly fixed pillars were made of concrete in the shape of a truncated pyramid (base: 80 x 80 centimeters; upper surface: 40 x 40 centimeters; height: 75–80 centimeters; Fig. 78). In order to facilitate dismantling, pillars were wrapped with triple-folded foil coated with lubricant. Concrete foundations were laid below the footing of the Late Roman/Byzantine walls.

Tracing and leveling of both constructions was carried out by means of theodolite surveying with a mean accuracy of $\pm$ 0.5 centimeters.

Roof Structure

The roof structure, based on a 3 x 3 meter module, was made of truss girders 12 meters long, constructed of welded steel 2 x ⌊50 x 50 x 5 according to computer made calculations (Fig. 78). Trusses (h_{max} = 1.2 m; h_{min} = 0.6 m) were fixed at 3 meter intervals along the east–west axis. In order to avoid erecting costly and troublesome scaffoldings over mosaic floors, halves of workshop-prefabricated trusses were joined on

Fig. 80: Moving assembled trusses to their final positions.

Fig. 81: Final stage of roof construction.

the small assembling platform (2 x 3 meters) constructed close to the shelter's eastern wall, exactly between the beams.

The level of the platform, even with the roof-supporting beams, greatly facilitated the whole operation and ensured necessary accuracy. Assembled trusses, weighing approximately 300 kg, were then moved in vertical position to prescribed locations.

Vertical braces joining trusses in the level of the roof ridge were made of steel angles ⌊40. Horizontal braces, in the outer eastern and western sections of the roof, in the plane of upper bands were made of similar angles ⌊40. Purloins spaced at 1 meter were made of channel bars ⌊80 welded to the upper members of the trusses (Fig. 78).

Roofing

The roof was covered with corrugated iron sheets (6 x 1 meters, 0.6 millimeters thick). Sheets were coated with beige varnish and bolted every 20 centimeters in lines set 3 meters apart.

Thermal insulation was made of hard Styrofoam sheets (2 x 1 meters and 4 centimeters thick) inserted into channels.

Roof gable walls were made of smoked glass panels (8 millimeters thick and 1 meter long) in conformity with the basic division of panel glass walls. Buttings of trusses from the south and north were screened with a strip of corrugated sheet iron. Gutters were fixed on both roof edges. Both outlets of the gutters were equipped with stone gargoyles.

The western and eastern edges of the roof were screened with beige painted wooden planks.

It was decided to abandon the original idea of constructing a ceiling, and to leave the steel structure of the roof exposed. Immediately below the roofing, 10 steel angles (30 x 30 millimeters, 15 meters long) were welded to purloins in order to fix thermal insulation in the form of hard Styrofoam sheets. The gap between top purloins was screened from below with a strip of sheet iron.

Mounts of the gutters were welded along the northern and southern edges of the roof. They were made in accordance with the adopted gradient of drainage, the length of each mount varying from 10 to 30 centimeters. Stone outlets were fixed on the eastern end of the gutters.

Niche Construction

The Expanded Statement of Work approved the incorporation of the newly discovered mosaic under the protection of the specially designed shelter niche. The technical design for the shelter niche (3.5 meters wide and 2 meters deep) was prepared and necessary construction work was completed according to the guidelines set in the Expanded Statement of Work. The niche was formed following the dismantling of a section of the southern wall of the Late Roman/Byzantine Building B which had been entirely reconstructed in the 1970s. The construction of the niche increased the exhibition space of the shelter in the southeastern direction.

The construction work was carried out between January 25 and March 7, 1999.

Southern Revetment Wall

The engineering review of the site pointed to the crucial necessity of recessing the revetment wall deeper into the escarpment. The escarpment behind the discovered mosaic reaches the height of 6 meters above the floor level. Taking these conditions into account, the option of using the existing southern wall of the shelter niche was rejected. A newly built structure of such a height made of relatively small stones would not be able to sustain the considerable load of the escarpment. Therefore, a decision was taken to build a southern wall for the niche (3.5 x 3.4 meters) as a reinforced concrete wall (about 25–30 centimeters thick) in front of the existing one. Such a wall stabilizes the slope by transferring the horizontal thrust onto the side walls of the niche, effectively buttressing the whole unit (Figs. 75 and 82).

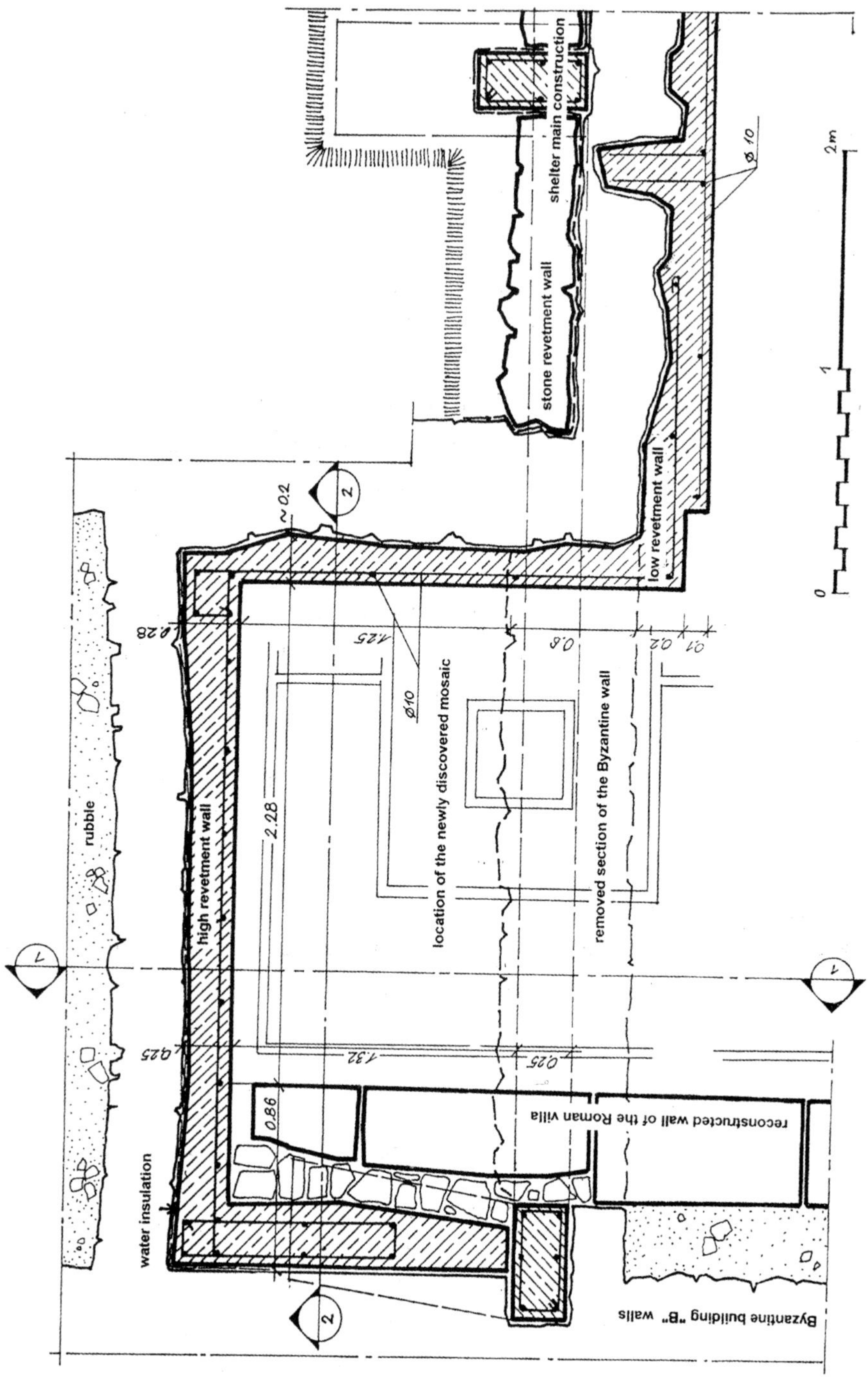

Fig. 82: Niche construction, ground plan, lower level. (Drawing by W. Kołątaj)

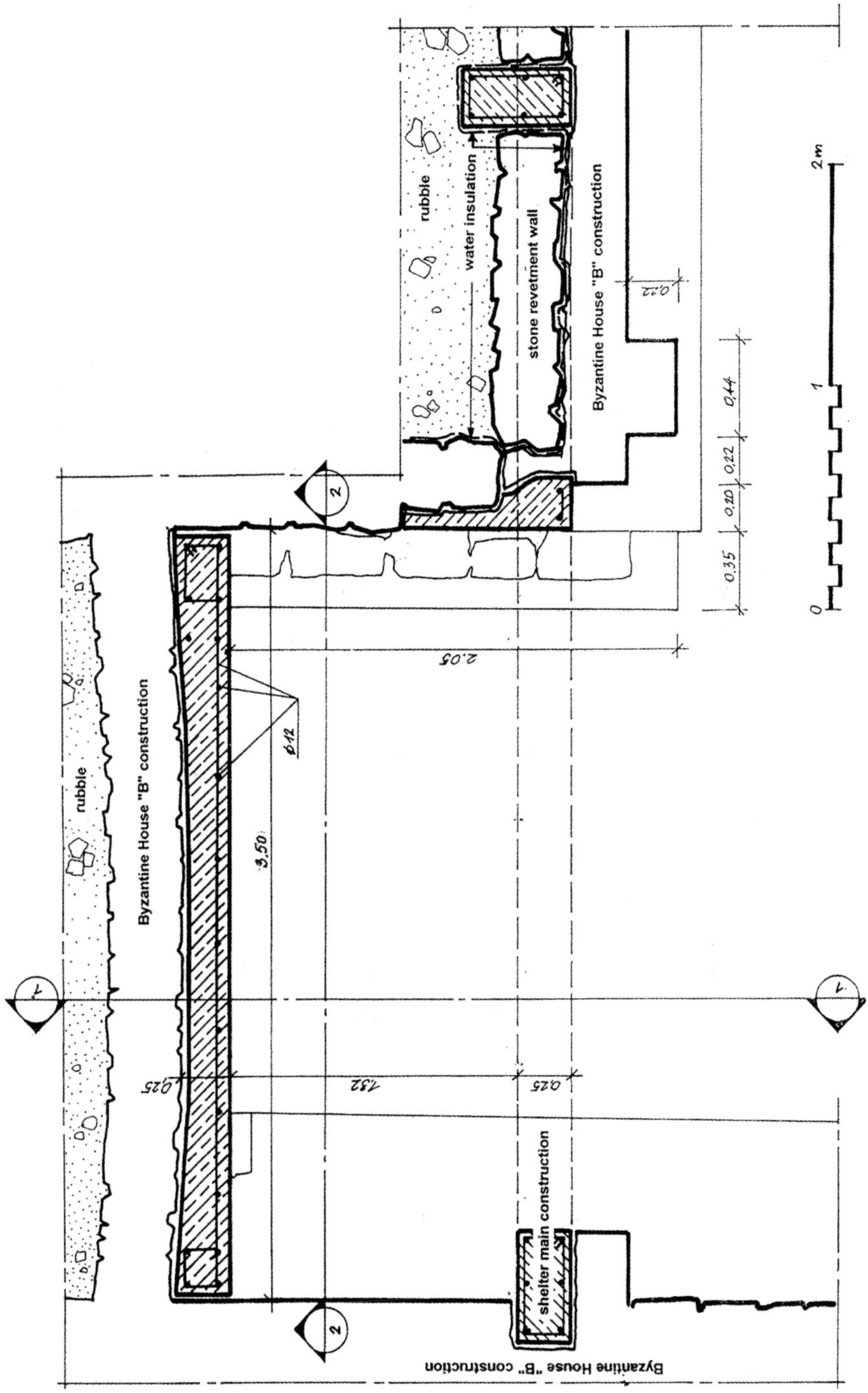

Fig. 83: Niche construction, ground plan, upper level. (Drawing by W. Kołątaj)

Fig. 84: Byzantine wall set over mosaic in Room 6.

The lower section of the revetment wall was additionally keyed to perpendicular concrete buttresses. The eastern buttress (1.3 meters high) was concealed behind a restored wall of the Early Roman Villa *alpha*. The western one (1 meter high) also serves as an encasing wall, screening the foundations of the Late Roman/Byzantine House B walls founded upon rubble (see Fig. 82).

Side walls

Both the eastern and western walls of the niche were formed by sections of ancient walls of the Late Roman/Byzantine House B. Additional reinforced concrete beams set on the top of those walls function as buttresses of the southern revetment wall in its upper level. Both beams abut the two concrete pillars of the main construction of the shelter.

Ceiling

The niche was covered with a reinforced concrete ceiling slab (20 centimeters thick) placed 3.4 meters above the mosaics' level and set on top of the south revetment wall and the side beams (Figs. 85 and 86). An empty space (1.06 meters high), between the niche ceiling and the beam supporting the entire structure of the shelter's roof from the south, was closed with a thin concrete wall. Such a construction enabled the extension of the slope over the niche, burying it in the adjacent escarpment. The general shape of the shelter roof remained unchanged.

Damp-proofing

Behind the revetment wall of the niche there exists a wall, reconstructed in 1973, badly warped in both horizontal and vertical directions. On the northern surface of that wall, two layers of thick polystyrene foil were firmly pressed to the back surface of the concrete revetment wall (see Fig. 78). The protective layer of foil was also laid under the foundation and on the top of the wall. Over the upper surface of the niche ceiling, a draining structure made of small stones joined with cement mortar was formed. This structure was made sloping 10 degrees toward the east. The upper surface of the structure, as well as the back surface of the front wall of the niche, were impregnated with ADDICON (an acrylic resin based compound) and covered with double foil sheets. This insulation, forming a U-shaped sloping surface (about 1.5 meters wide)

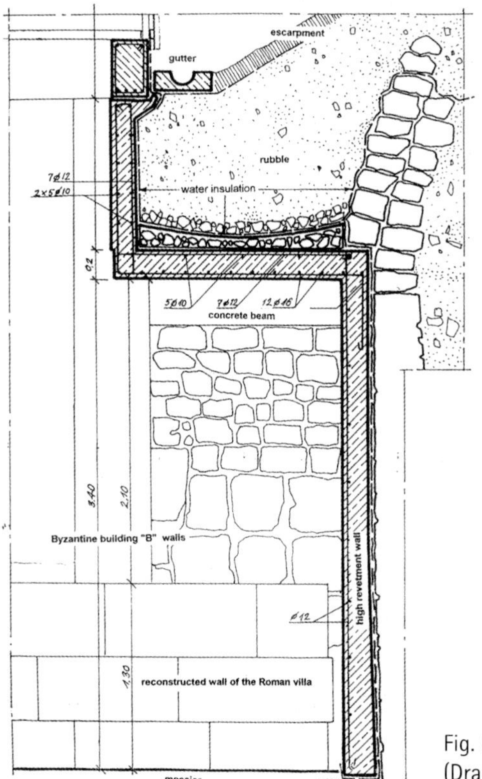

Fig. 85: Niche construction, section 1. (Drawing by W. Kołątaj)

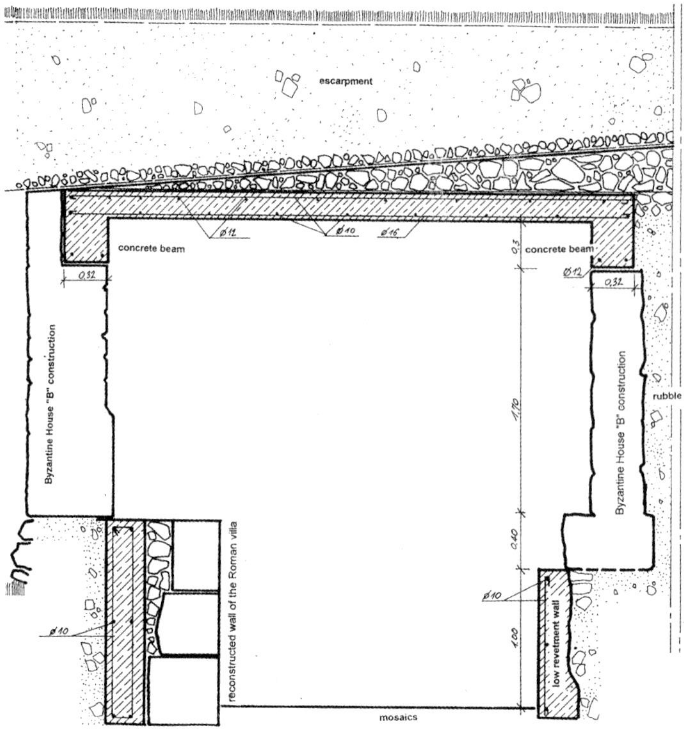

Fig. 86: Niche construction, section 2. (Drawing by W. Kołątaj)

behind the entire southern wall of the shelter, protects the whole construction against heavy rains and surface flooding.

Over the ceiling of the niche, along the southern edge of the shelter, a new stone revetment wall has been built. The said wall, built on top of the southern wall of the Late Roman/Byzantine House B, was structured without mortar, to slightly incline to the south. This structure was designed not only in order to shape a proper waterproof gutter along the southern wall of the shelter, but also to counteract horizontal and vertical thrust of the escarpment (Fig. 86).

Panel Glass Walls

The interior of the shelter is naturally illuminated from the east, north, and west. The glass wall was constructed entirely of security glass panels 1 centimeter thick, fixed on the top and the bottom only. No additional vertical fittings were employed.

The main entrance to the shelter is at the northern wall (5.8 x 3.1 meters) between the remains of Late Roman/Byzantine Buildings F and B. A glass swing door with a ventilation window above were positioned at the western end of this wall. The northern glass wall has been divided by a horizontal bar fixed at the level of 2.1 meters above the ground and a vertical bar placed 94 centimeters off the wall of the Late Roman/Byzantine Building F. These bars mark the position of the door and window.

Adjoining Rooms E1, E2, E3, and E4 of the Late Roman/Byzantine building were adapted as an exit patio (about 36 square meters) of the shelter (Fig. 6). A green garden patio was embellished with a palm tree and equipped with benches (Figs. 66 and 74). Ivy or other climbers will be introduced on the northern wall of Building D. The panel glass wall (6 x 3.5 meters), with the exit door and ventilation window, encloses the shelter from the east. This large glass surface incorporates the remains of the Late Roman/Byzantine wall dividing Houses E and F. For construction reasons, the glass wall was divided by a horizontal steel frame measuring 8 x 4 centimeters set at 2 meters above ground level. Smoked glass panels fill the gables.

An irregularly shaped window panel fills the entire surface above the preserved eastern wall of the Late Roman/Byzantine building. Gables are closed with smoked glass panels. Vertical divisions of panels continue in both sections of the glass wall (Figs. 70 and 75).

One glass panel under the horizontal frame was fixed as hopper windows, opening along the vertical axis. This feature ensures better ventilation of the shelter. Rim latches with side bolts were installed. Lower edges of the panels were equipped with drips.

Footbridge Construction

The footbridge, placed approximately 1 meter above the level of the mosaics, enables visitors to walk around, view, and photograph mosaics without stepping on them and damaging them. It follows an angular path between the entrance and the exit and is positioned directly over the walls forming the southern and eastern limits of the *triclinium*. The level of the footbridge is three steps lower than the entrance platform and the exit.

The footbridge was constructed as a frame made of double steel eye bars (180 millimeters) fixed 40 centimeters apart, welded together to form a T-shape structure (Fig. 88). The frame composed of two perpendicular sections (12 meters and 6.80 meters respectively) rests on partially restored ancient walls of the villa. The 80 centimeter wide flooring is assembled of wooden planks in sections 1.5 meters long and 5 centimeters thick, supported by T-irons (50 x 50 millimeters) welded perpendicularly to the frame.

The width of the bridge enables the undisturbed traffic of visitors moving in single file. The railing is made of U-shaped steel pipes (3.8

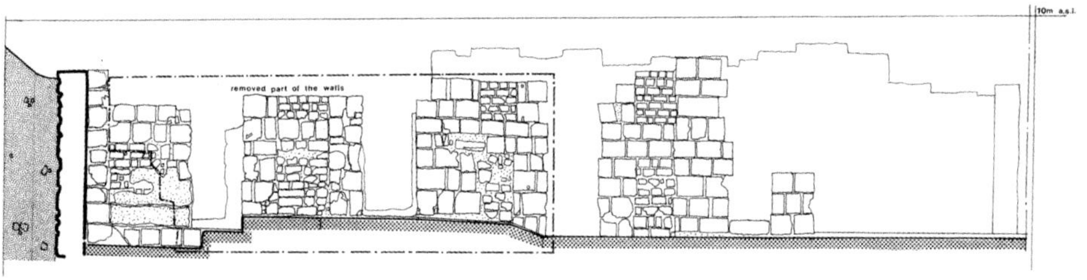

Fig. 87: Building F, dismantled wall adjoining courtyard, eastern elevation. (Drawing by W. Kołątaj)

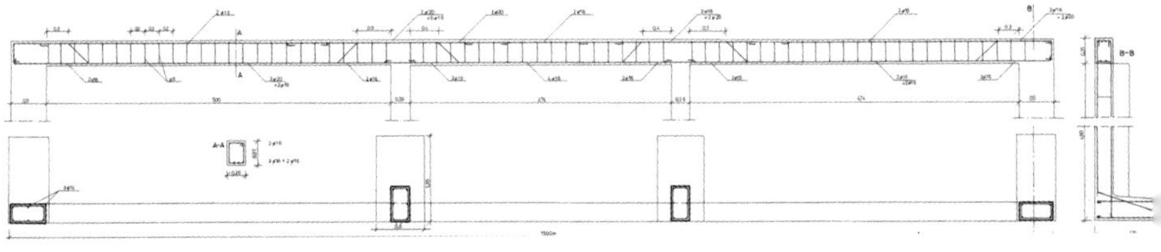
Fig. 88: Footbridge construction. (Drawing by W. Kołątaj)

centimeters in diameter) welded to the structural frame in equal distances (1.5–2 meters). Instead of a traditional handrail, a steel wire (j 6 mm) has been stretched on two levels between the railing posts. Such wire railing is visually unobtrusive, it does not block the view of the mosaics, and it discourages leaning on it.

Drainage System

The mosaic floors are situated at the lowest point of the excavations, about 1.80 meters below the surrounding area. As the mosaic floors lie significantly below the level of the nearby modern city sewage system, draining water from the area of the exhibition poses a challenge. As it was considered impractical to install a mechanical pumping system, the only other solution was to take advantage of the ancient sewage system surviving on the site. The ancient sewage system running along the R4 street had already been partially cleared and successfully used for draining. After some sections of the ancient canals had been cleared, they were turned into a single system draining off rainwater from the escarpment and from ground level. The rainwater from the roof will be drained off to the nearby wells and underground cistern. Both wells reach the subsoil water table. In case of overflow, the cistern will be used as a standby reservoir (Fig. 65).

Given the relatively limited dimensions of the roof combined with good soil permeability and grass growing on the surrounding slopes, the whole area will be sufficiently protected against inundation.

The construction of the shelter was carried out using solely locally produced materials, including building materials, trusses, security glass, and fittings. Local manpower and direct supervision of work were the main factors contributing to its cost effectiveness.

Glossary

amphora: ancient Greek jar or vase having a large oval body, narrow cylindrical neck, and two handles that rise almost to the level of the mouth.

band: continuous linear motif composed of 4 or more rows of tesserae.

bichrome: mosaic design made in two colors, usually black on white background.

***cubiculum*:** the bedroom in a Roman house.

***emblema*:** decorative figural panel, prepared separately and inserted into mosaic.

filet: continuous linear motif made of 1–3 rows of tesserae.

***hederae*:** decorative element in the form of stylized ivy leaf.

insula: an ancient Roman building or a group of buildings standing together forming a block or square and usually constituting an apartment building.

koine: a dialect or language of a region, country, or people that has become the common or standard language of a larger area and of other peoples.

lacuna: missing fragment of mosaic.

nucleus: upper waterproof layer of mortar composed of crushed pottery, ground stone, and ashes mixed with mortar.

oikos: household.

opus isodomum: A masonry pattern in which stones of uniform length and uniform height are set so that each vertical joint is centered over the block beneath. Horizontal joints are continuous and the vertical joints form discontinuous straight lines. *(Cyril Harris Dictionary of Architecture and Construction)*

opus sectile: mosaic floor execution technique using stone slabs (most often marble) cut to different shapes and sizes, arranged in ornamental patterns.

opus tesselatum: mosaic floor execution technique using small cubes (tesserae) arranged in geometric or figural motifs and patterns.

opus vermiculatum: variant of the *opus tesselatum* technique employing exceptionally fine cubes (with each side less than 5 mm), used most often for figural designs and emblemas.

peristyle: colonnaded court of the house.

rudus: lower layer of bedding composed of broken stone, usually mixed with mortar.

semis: orthogonal composition consisting of repeated ornamental elements that are not adjoining, but appear at regular intervals.

setting bed: layer of lime with marble powder or lime with sand and ashes; the tesserae were pressed into this layer.

statumen: strongly stamped ground evened with rubble or rough stone underneath the mortar bedding.

tessera: small stone, glass, or terracotta cube used in the making of tessellated pavements.

triclinium: the dining room in a Roman house.

Notes

1. L. Dąbrowski, "Résume des recherches archéologiques faites autour du Fort Kôm al-Dikka." *Bulletin de Faculté des Lettres, Université d'Alexandrie* 14: 39–49 (1960).
2. The street designation system for ancient Alexandria was introduced by Mahmud Bey al-Falaki in the nineteenth century. In keeping with this still-used convention, the longitudinal streets running from east to west are marked with the letter L and successive numbers. The north–south streets are marked as R followed by successive numbers, starting from the eastern end of the city (Mahmud Bey al-Falaki, *Mémoire sur l'antique Alexandrie*. Copenhagen: Impr. de Bianco Luno, 1872).
3. W. Kołątaj, *Imperial Baths at Kom al-Dikka* (Warsaw: Centre d'Archéologie Méditerranéenne de l'Académie Polonaise des Sciences, 1992).
4. B. Tkaczow and I. Zych, *The Topography of Ancient Alexandria: An Archaeological Map* (Warsaw: Zakład Archeologii Śródziemnomorskiej, Polskiej Akadmii Nauk, 1993), 85–112.
5. M. Rodziewicz, *Les habitations romaines tardives d'Alexandrie à la lumiere des fouilles polonaises à Kôm al-Dikka* (Warsaw: Éditions

scientifiques de Pologne, 1984); G. Majcherek, "Notes on Alexandrian Habitat: Roman and Byzantine Houses from Kom al-Dikka," *Topoi* 5, no. 1 (1995): 133–50.

6. M. Rodziewicz, *Les habitations romaines*, 143.
7. M. Rodziewicz, "Un quartier d'habitation gréco-romain à Kôm al-Dikka," *Études et Travaux*, no. 9 (1976): 198–202; M. Rodziewicz, *Les habitations romaines*, 128–40.
8. M. Rodziewicz, *Les habitations romaines*, 148–59.
9. Fig. 4; G. Majcherek, "The Late Roman Ceramics from Sector 'G' (Alexandria 1986–1987)," *Études et Travaux*, no. 16 (1992): 82–116; G. Majcherek, "Gazan Amphorae: Typology Reconsidered," eds. H. Meyza and J. Młynarczyk in *Hellenistic and Roman Pottery in the Eastern Mediterranean, Advances in Scientific Studies.* (Warsaw: Research Center for Mediterranean Archaeology, Polish Academy of Sciences, 1995), 169, Pls. 7–8, form 4.
10. Fig. 5:5; M. Egloff, *Kellia: La poterie Copte; quatre siècles d'artisanat et d'échanges en Basse-Égypte* (Geneva: Georg, 1977), 115–16, Pl. 59: 3–4, 6.
11. Fig. 5:3; J.W. Hayes, *Late Roman Pottery* (London: British School at Rome, 1972).
12. Ibid.
13. Fig. 5:2, 5:6; J.-Y. Empereur and M. Picon, "Les régions de production d'amphores impériales en Méditerranée orientale," in *Anfore Romane e storia economica: un decennio di ricerche* (Rome: École Française de Rome, 1989), 236–43; D. Pieri, "Les importations d'amphores orientales en Gaule méridionale durant l'Antiquité tardive et le Haut-Moyen Age (IVe–VIIe siècles après J.-C): Typologie, chronologie et contenu," in *Société française d'étude de la céramique antique en Gaule, Actes du Congrès d'Istres 21–24 mai 1998.* (Marseille: SFECAG, 1998), 97–106.
14. Fig. 5:1; Pieri, "Les importations."
15. D. Pieri, "Les importations."

16. Pl. 7; D.M. Bailey, *Roman Provincial Lamps.* Vol. 3 of *A Catalogue of the Lamps in the British Museum* (London: British Museum Publications, 1988), 226–29.
17. G. Majcherek, "Notes on Alexandrian Habitat," 137.
18. C. Saliou, *Les lois de bâtiments: Voisinage et habitat urbain dans l'empire romain* (Beirut: Institut français d'archéologie du Prôche-Orient, 1994).
19. M. Rodziewicz, *Les habitations romaines*, Pl. IX.
20. P. Pensabene, *Elementi architettonici di Alessandria e di altri siti egiziani*, Vol. 3, *Repertorio d'arte dell'Egitto greco-romano: Serie C* (Rome: "L'Erma" di Bretschneider, 1993), Pls. 92–99, 101; J. McKenzie, *The Architecture of Petra* (Oxford and New York: Oxford University Press, 1990), 73, Pls. 211–14; J. McKenzie, "The Architectural Style of Roman and Byzantine Alexandria and Egypt," in "Archaeological Research in Roman Egypt: The Proceedings of the Seventeenth Classical Colloquium of the Department of Greek and Roman Antiquities, British Museum, 1–4 December 1993," ed. D.M. Bailey, *Journal of Roman Archaeology*, Supplementary Series 19 (1996): 130–34, Figs. 1d and 4c.
21. J.W. Graham, "Origins and Interrelations of the Greek House and the Roman House," *Phoenix*, no. 20 (1966): 3–25.
22. M. Rodziewicz, "Un quartier d'habitation gréco-romain à Kôm al-Dikka," *Études et Travaux*, no. 9 (1976): 180.
23. M. Rodziewicz, *Les habitations romaines*, Fig. 31.
24. For the remnants of houses excavated throughout the city see A. Adriani, *Annuaire du Musée Gréco-Romain (1935–39)* (Alexandria: Musée Gréco-Romain d'Alexandrie, 1939), 24–54, 149–50; and B. Tkaczow and I. Zych, *Topography of ancient Alexandria.*
25. K. Michałowski, "Les fouilles polonaises a Tell Atrib," *Annales du Service des Antiquités de l'Égypte*, no. 58 (1958): 235–45.
26. W.A. Daszewski, "Témoignage de l'urbanisme de la côte méditerranéenne de l'Égypte à l'époque hellénistique et romaine à la

lumière des fouilles de Marina el-Alamein," *Bulletin de la Société Française d'Égyptologie*, no. 132 (1995): 19–25, Figs. 8–9.

27. M. Rodziewicz, "Remarks on the Domestic and Monastic Architecture in Alexandria and Surroundings," in ed. E.C.M. van den Brink *The Archaeology of the Nile Delta: Problems and Priorities* (Amsterdam: Netherlands Foundation for Archaeological Research in Egypt, 1988), 267–77.
28. A. Adriani, *Annuaire du Musée Gréco-Romain (1933–35)* (Alexandria: Musée Gréco-Romain d'Alexandrie, 1936).
29. G. Majcherek, "Alexandria 1994: Excavations," *Polish Archaeology in the Mediterranean*, no. 6 (1995): 15–18, Fig. 1.
30. J.-Y. Empereur and M. Picon, "Les ateliers d'amphores du lac Mariut," *Bulletin de Correspondance Hellénique*, Suppl. no. 33 (1998): Fig. 4.
31. Fig. 8: 1–2; Egloff, *Kellia*, 114, Pl. 59, 2; type 172.
32. G. Kapitän 1961: 276–318; S.J. Keay, *Late Roman Amphorae in the Western Mediterranean: A Typology and Economic Study; The Catalan Evidence* (Oxford: B.A.R, 1984), 136–39; Figs. 52–53.
33. H.S. Robinson, *Pottery of the Roman Period: Chronology*, Athenian Agora 5. (Princeton, N.J.: American School of Classical Studies at Athens, 1959), 17, F65–66; C. Panella, "Oriente ed Occidente: considerazioni su alcune anfore 'egee' di età imperiale a Ostia," *Bulletin de Correspondance Hellenique*, Suppl. no. 13 (1986): 614.
34. Fig. 8:5; A. Marangou-Lerat, *Le vin et les amphores de Crète de l'époque classique à l'époque impériale* (Athens: École française d'Athènes, 1995), 68–74.
35. Fig. 8:6; S. Keay, *Late Roman Amphorae.*
36. Fig. 8:7; C. Panella, "Appunti su uno grupo di anfore della prima, media e tarda età imperiale," in *Ostia III: le terme del nuotatore, scavo degli ambiente III, VI, VII, . . .* ; C. Panella and A. Carandini (Rome: De Luca, 1973), 460–633.
37. S. Keay, *Late Roman Amphorae.*

38. P.M. Fraser, "Byzantine Alexandria: Decline and Fall," *Bulletin de la Sociéte Archéologique d'Alexandrie*, no. 45 (1993): 91–106.
39. M. Rodziewicz, "Un quartier d'habitation," 192.
40. R. Ling, *Roman Painting* (Cambridge: Cambridge University Press, 1991), 2–22.
41. H.S. Robinson, *Pottery of the Roman Period*, 48; Panella, "Oriente ed Occidente," 610–11.
42. Obv. Laureate head to the right. Legend : AVTKAI [CTPAIAN ADPI-ANOCCEB]. Rev. Helmeted Athena standing left, holding spear in left hand and two corn-ears in the right one. Minted in Alexandria in the 17th year of reign (AD 132/133). Cf. A. Geissen, *Katalog alexandrinischer Kaisermünzen der Sammlung des Instituts für Altertumskunde der Universität zu Köln*, vol. 2 (Opladen: Westdeutscher Verlag, 1978), no. 1072. All the coins were identified by Dr. Barbara Lichocka, to whom I am indebted for assistance.
43. Obv. Laureate bust to the right. Rev. Athena and Ares standing. 18th year of reign (AD 114/115), cf. A. Geissen, *Katalog Alexandrinischer*, no. 668.
44. A. Adriani, *Annuaire du Musée Gréco-Romain (1933–35)*, 27.
45. M. Rodziewicz, "Un quartier d'habitation"; Rodziewicz, *Les habitations romaines*, 43–53.
46. For a general introduction, see R. Ling, *Ancient Mosaics* (London: British Museum Press, 1998) and K. Dunbabin, *Mosaics of the Greek and Roman World* (Cambridge: Cambridge University Press, 1999). For geometric motifs, M. Blanchard et al., "Répertoire graphique du décor géométrique dans la mosaïque antique," *Bulletin de l'Association Internationale pour l'Étude de la Mosaïque Antique*, May 1973, and C. Balmelle et al., *Le décor géométrique de la mosaïque romaine: Répertoire graphique et descriptif des compositions linéaires et isotropes* (Paris: Picard, 1985) are used, and for the acanthus scroll border the code devised by Dauphin (C. Dauphin, "A New Method of Studying Early Byzantine Mosaic Pavements [Coding and a Computed Cluster Analysis] with Special Reference to the

Levant," *Levant* no. 8 [1976]: 113–49). I am greatly indebted to Prof. Claudine Dauphin for her invaluable comments on the subject.

47. M. Blanchard et al., "Répertoire," no. 110.
48. M. Blanchard et al., "Répertoire," no. 543, diameter 1.22 meters, 6 centimeters wide.
49. C. Balmelle et al., *Décor*, Pl. 1t, 4 centimeters wide.
50. M. Blanchard et al., "Répertoire," no. 544.
51. C. Balmelle et al., *Décor*, Pl. 113 g, h.
52. For similar motif, see D. Levi, *Antioch Mosaic Pavements* (Princeton: Princeton University Press, 1947), 205, Fig. 77.
53. M. Rodziewicz, *Les habitations romaines*, 35–36, Fig. 19.
54. The technical quality of mosaic is best described by measuring a number of tesserae within a square area of 10 x 10 centimeters (=1 square decimeter).
55. W.A. Daszewski, *Corpus of Mosaics from Egypt 1. Hellenistic and Early Roman Period* (Mainz: P. von Zabern, 1985), 29, note 14.
56. M. Rodziewicz, "Un quartier d'habitation," Fig. 10.
57. Blanchard et al., "Répertoire," no. 14.
58. Pl. 17; Balmelle et al., *Décor*, Pl. 108c.
59. A similar motif, although with counterchanged colors, can be seen on a mosaic floor from Gabbari, dated to the second half of the first century BC. Cf. Daszewski, *Corpus*, 122.
60. C. Balmelle et al., *Décor*, Pl. 1i.
61. C. Balmelle et al., *Décor*, Pl. 1y; 5 centimeters wide.
62. Pl. 18; Balmelle et al., *Décor*, Pl. 15a.
63. For a discussion of the use of such bedding, see F. Guidobaldi, *Sectilia pavimenta di Villa Adriana* (Rome: Istituto poligrafico e Zecca dello Stato, 1994), 49–55.
64. P. Pensabene and P. Arthur, *Marmi antichi: Problemi d'impiego, di restauro e d'identificazione* (Rome: "L'Erma" di Bretschneider, 1985).
65. G. Majcherek, "The Late Roman Ceramics," 18.
66. A.-M. Guimier-Sorbets, "Le pavement du triclinium à la Méduse

dans une maison d'époque impériale à Alexandrie," *Alexandrina*, no. 1 (1998): 115–40.

67. Ibid.

68. The few known examples of *opus sectile* mosaic floors from Egypt decorated rooms serving other purposes, cf. roundel from Kom Trouga, decorating a bath and dated to the late first century BC (A. Khachab, "Les hammams du Kom Trougah," *Annales du Service des Antiquités de l'Égypte*, no. 54 (1957): 117ff.); and a mosaic floor discovered in the Late Roman *hospitium* in Huwariya (second half of the fifth century AD) (M. Rodziewicz "Opus sectile mosaics from Alexandria and Mareotis," in *Tesserae: Festschrift für Josef Engemann*, ed. Josef Engemann (Münster: Aschendorff, 1991), 208–11, Figs. 4–7. Another fragmentarily preserved, fine mosaic floor was discovered at Kom al-Dikka in the neighboring Early Roman House *gamma* (third century AD), but it does not appear to have had a tessellated border (M. Rodziewicz, "Opus sectile mosaics," Fig. 2). Fragments of marble floors with *opus sectile* elements were also found in the triclinium of an Early Roman villa uncovered under the Theatre Portico (G. Majcherek, "Alexandria 1994,"11–13, Fig. 1) and in the House F (G. Majcherek, "Kom al-Dikka, Excavations 1996–1997," *Polish Archaeology in the Mediterranean*, no. 9 (1998): 27–28, Fig. 2). A small section of *opus sectile* pavement was found also in the vestibule of the Theater (W. Kołątaj and T. Kołataj, "Polish Excavations at Kom al-Dikka in Alexandria, 1967," *Bulletin de la Société Archéologique d'Alexandrie*, no. 43 (1975): Pl. 8). The popularity of such floors in Roman Alexandria is evidenced also by numerous finds of loose profiled marble slabs all over the site. Alexandrian workshops are believed to have produced the glass *opus sectile* panels found at Kenchrae (L. Ibrahim et al., "The Panels of Opus Sectile in Glass," in *Kenchreai, Eastern Port of Corinth: Results of Investigations by the University of Chicago and Indiana University for the American School of Classical Studies at Athens*

(Leiden: Brill, 1976). Similar glass panels have been discovered also at Antinoe (H.W. Müller, "Koptische Glasintarsien mit figürlichen Darstellungen aus Antinoe/Mittelägypten," *Pantheon*, no. 20 (1962).

69. G. Pesce, *Il 'Palazzo delle Colonne' in Tolemaide di Cirenaica* (Rome: "L'Erma" di Bretschneider, 1950), 38, Fig. 42.
70. C.H. Kraeling, *Ptolemais, City of the Libyan Pentapole* (Chicago: University of Chicago Press, 1962), 138, Figs. 68–69, Pl. 49A.
71. P. Mingazzini and E. Fiandra, *L'insula di Giasone Magno a Cirene* (Rome: "L'Erma" di Bretschneider, 1966).
72. J.A. Lloyd, ed., *Excavations at Sidi Khrebish Benghazi (Berenice)* Vol. 1., Supplements to Libya Antiqua V (Tripoli: Dept. of Antiquities, Ministry of Teaching and Education, L.A.R., 1978), 156–58, Pl. XIIb; Michaelides 1998.
73. M. Alexander and M. Ennaifer, "Quelques précisions à propos de la chronologie des mosaïques d'Utique," in *La Mosaïque Gréco-Romaine II: Actes du IIème Colloque international pour l'étude de la mosaïque antique (Vienne, 30 août–4 septembre 1971)*, Pl. XIII, 2 (Paris: A. and J. Picard, 1975).
74. C. Balmelle et al., *Décor*, Pl. 141a.
75. M. Blanchard et al., "Répertoire," IIIa3.
76. C. Balmelle et al., *Décor*, Pl. 70j. For the popularity of polychrome guilloche motif framing either single decorative panels or the entire composition on the Roman mosaics from North Africa cf. second century mosaic from the House of Dionysiac Procession from El-Djem (M. Blanchard-Lemée et al., *Sols de l'Afrique Romain, Mosaïques de Tunisie* (Paris: Imprimerie Nationale, 1995), Fig. 58) and from Zliten, (S. Aurigemma, *Tripolitania. I monumenti d'arte decorative: I mosaici* (Rome: Istituto poligrafico dello Stato, 1960), Pls. 126–29). Cf. also other examples from Utica, Bulla Regia (House of the Treasury), Timgad, Sabratha and Leptis Magna. In the East, the motif is attested on numerous floors from Antioch, Apamea and Palestinian sites cf. detailed references in C. Dauphin, "Une mosaïque de la 'Renaissance

justinienne' en Galilée occidentale," in "Fifth International Colloquium on Ancient Mosaics," ed. R. Ling, *Journal of Roman Archaeology* Supplementary Series 9, Part 2 (1995): 108–109.

77. See H. Heinzel, R. Fitter and J. Parslow, *Birds of Britain and Europe with North Africa and the Middle East*, 2nd ed. (London: HarperCollins, 1995), 126.
78. See H. Heinzel et al., *Birds of Britain and Europe.*
79. C. Balmelle et al., *Décor*, Pl. 15a.
80. On the use of colored glass and faience cubes in mosaics see A.-M. Guimier-Sorbets and M.-D. Nenna, "L'emploi du verre, de la faïence et de la peinture dans les mosaïques de Délos," *Bulletin de Correspondance Hellénique*, no. 16 (1992): 607–31; on the chromatic development of mosaics see also Daszewski 1983: 161–65.
81. Until now, aside from the mosaic floors from Kom al-Dikka, there were only three other examples of figural mosaic floors known from Alexandria (see W.A. Daszewski, "From Hellenistic Polychromy of Sculptures to Roman Mosaics," in *Alexandria and Alexandrinism: Papers Delivered at a Symposium Organized by the J. Paul Getty Museum 22–25 April 1993*, ed. Kenneth Hamma, 146–47 (Malibu, California: The J. Paul Getty Museum, 1996)). Another new example belonging to this category is the floor with a Medusa head discovered during French excavations at the Diana Theatre in 1994 (A.-M. Guimier-Sorbets, "Le pavement du triclinium," 115–40).
82. On the mosaic floor from Thmuis, birds constitute part of a Nilotic landscape decoration. The piece of mosaic floor from Canopus (Abu Kir) is also interpreted as part of a Nilotic scene (E. Breccia, *Monuments de l'Égypte Gréco-Romain* (Bergamo: Officini dell'Istituto italiano d'arti grafiche, 1926), 43, 82, pl. 47, 3–4; Cf. Daszewski, *Corpus*, 136–38, cat. nos. 30, 32).
83. The design was already known in the Western Mediterranean in the first century AD and became particularly popular in the second and

third centuries AD. For bibliographic references to African and Italian sites see S. Gozlan, "Les mosaïques," in *La maison du triomphe de Neptune à Acholla (Botria, Tunisie)* (Rome: École Française de Rome, 1992), 160. Compositions of this kind are used most frequently to decorate rooms of secondary importance, like corridors, passages, cubicula, etc.

84. P. Bruneau, *Les mosaïques*, Vol. 29 of *Exploration archéologique de Délos* (Paris: Éditions de Boccard, 1972).
85. M. Rodziewicz, "Un quartier d'habitation."
86. C. Balmelle et al., *Décor*, Pl. 1y, 5 centimeters wide.
87. C. Balmelle et al., *Décor*, Pl. 232c.
88. C. Balmelle et al., *Décor*, Pl. 1y.
89. C. Dauphin, "A New Method," code type $AoII_2$ c; Balmelle et al., *Décor*, Pl. 64e.
90. Similar scrollwork, but more elaborate in color and graphic design, is frequent on African mosaic floors, some also connected with Dionysiac themes, see mosaic from Thysdrus (al-Djem) depicting Dionysius riding a tiger (Blanchard-Lemée et al., *Sols de l'Afrique Romain*, 86) and Mosaic of the Four Seasons (ibid., 45 and 86) and mosaic floor from Thuburbo Maius (ibid., Fig. 213). Acanthus scroll decoration so popular in the Imperial time gave way to the vine scrolls in the Late Roman/Byzantine period, though this decorative tradition apparently survived on Coptic textiles and sculpture. Cf. C. Dauphin, "The Development of the 'Inhabited Scroll' in Architectural Sculpture and Mosaic Art From Late Imperial Times to the Seventh Century AD," *Levant* no. 19 (1987): 185, particularly notes 18 and 25, with further references to the Egyptian monuments.
91. Guimier-Sorbets and Nenna, "L'emploi du verre."
92. A similar design, while absent from Egyptian floors, is a fairly widespread motif in the Imperial mosaic decoration of the second century AD. It is rather rare in Africa in this period, (see Gozlan, "Les mosaïques," 24, bibliography of African sites) while frequent in

Antioch, (Levi, *Antioch Mosaic Pavements*, Pls. XIVa, XXVIIb, XLVIIa) and in Cyprus (see D. Michaelides, *Cypriot Mosaics*, Rev. ed. (Nicosia: Department of Antiquities, Cyprus, 1992), 27, Figs. 10a–b, panels of the Dioscuri from the House of Dionysus in Paphos; 86, Fig. 47, panel of Ktisis from Kourion).

93. An *emblema* fragment depicting Dionysus was also found during Polish excavations on Kom al-Dikka, see K. Kołodziejczyk, "Private Roman Bath at Kom al-Dikka in Alexandria," *Études et Travaux*, no. 2 (1968): 144–54, Fig. 5; and Daszewski, *Corpus*, 132–34, cat no. 23, Pl. 24c.
94. M. Blanchard-Lemée et al., *Sols de l'Afrique Romain*, Fig. 148.
95. I am very grateful to Prof. Daszewski for having drawn my attention to those scenes. In his opinion, the original fine central panel of the mosaic α-6 seemed to be deliberately changed from a hunting scene to a more Dionysiac theme of tamed animal. See also representations of a panther drinking from *kantharos* to be seen in the scene of Dionysiac cortége on the mosaic from Sousse (Blanchard-Lemée et al., *Sols de l'Afrique Romain*, Fig. 64), and on the mosaic from Constantine (K. Dunbabin, *The Mosaics of Roman North Africa: Studies in Iconography and Patronage* (Oxford: Clarendon Press, 1978) Fig. 174.
96. On the emblemata generally, see A. Balil, "ta. Estudios sobre mosaicos romanos IV," *Studia archeologica*, no. 39 (1976): 5–27; see also useful discussion based primarily on an analysis of ancient written sources, Daszewski, *Corpus*, 15–22.
97. M. Rodziewicz, *Les habitations romaines*, Fig. 31.
98. The same concept was employed in the display of ancient architecture in Stazione Termini in Rome.

Bibliography

Adriani, A. 1936. *Annuaire du Musée Gréco-Romain (1933–35).* Alexandria.

______. 1939. *Annuaire du Musée Gréco-Romain (1935–39).* Alexandria.

______. 1966. *Repertorio d'arte dell'Egitto Greco-Romano,* Serie C, vols. I–II, Palermo.

Alexander, M. and M. Ennaifer. 1971. "Quelques précisions a propos de la chronologie des mosaïques d'Utique." *La Mosaïque Gréco-Romaine,* II. Vienna: 31–39.

AISCOM 1996. *AISCOM–Atti del IV Colloquio del assoziazione Italiane per lo studio e la conservazione del mosaico.* Palermo: Edizioni del Girasole, 1996.

Aurigemma, S. 1960. *L'Italia in Africa. Tripolitania. I monumenti d'arte decorative: I mosaici.* Rome.

Bailey, D.M. 1988. *A Catalogue of the Lamps in the British Museum III, Roman Provincial Lamps.* London.

Balil, A. 1976. "Emblemata. Estudios sobre mosaicos romanos IV." *Studia archeologica* 39: 5–27.

Balmelle, C., M. Blanchard-Lemée, J.Christophe, J.-P. Darmon, A.-M. Guimier-Sorbets, H. Lavagne, R. Prudhomme, and. H. Stern, 1985. *Le décor géométrique de la mosaïque romaine: Répertoire graphique et descriptif des compositions linéaires et isotropes.* Paris.

Blanchard, M., J. Christophe, J.-P. Darmon, H. Lavagne, R. Prudhomme, H. Stern. 1973. "Répertoire graphique du décor géométrique dans la mosaïque antique." *Bulletin de l'Association Internationale pour l'Etude da la Mosaïque antique*, 4e Fascicule, May, Paris.

Blanchard-Lemée, M., M. Ennaifer, H. Slim, L. Slim, and G. Mermet. 1995. *Sols de l'Afrique Romain, Mosaïques de Tunisie*. Paris.

Breccia, E. 1926. *Monuments de l'Egypte Gréco-Romain*. Bergamo.

Bruneau, P. 1972. *Les mosaïques: Exploration archéologique de Délos*, vol. 29. Paris.

Chlouveraki, S. 1997. Mosaic Conservation. *Minerva-The International Review of Ancient Art and Archaeology* 8, 1: 36–39.

Dąbrowski, L. 1960. "Résume des recherches archéologiques faites autour du Fort Kôm al-Dikka." *Bulletin de Faculté des Lettres, Université d'Alexandrie* 14: 39–49.

Daszewski, W.A.D. 1983. "Notes on topography of Ptolemaic Alexandria." *Aleksandria e il Mondo ellenistico-Romano, Studi in onore di Achille Adriani, Studi e Materiali 4*. Rome.

———. 1985. *Corpus of Mosaics from Egypt I, Hellenistic and Early Roman Period*. Mainz.

———. 1995. "Témoignage de l'urbanisme de la côte méditerranéenne de l'Egypte à l'époque hellénistique et romaine à la lumière des fouilles de Marina el-Alamein." *Bulletin de la Société Française d'Égyptologie* 132: 11–29.

Daszewski, W.A. 1996. From Hellenistic Polychromy of Sculptures to Roman Mosaics, in *Alexandria and Alexandrinism: Papers Delivered at a Symposium Organized by The J. Paul Getty Museum April 1993*: 141–52.

Dauphin, C. 1976. "A New Method of Studying Early Byzantine Mosaic Pavements (Coding and a Computed Cluster Analysis) with Special Reference to the Levant." *Levant* 8: 113–49.

———. 1987. "The Development of the 'Inhabited Scroll' in Architectural Sculpture and Mosaic Art From Late Imperial Times to the Seventh Century AD." *Levant* 19: 183–212.

______. 1995. "Une mosaïque de la 'Renaissance justinienne' en Galilée occidentale," in *Fifth International Colloquium on Ancient Mosaics. Journal of Roman Archaeology Supplementary Series 9*, Part 2 (1995), ed. R. Ling: 101–12.

Dunbabin, K.M.D. 1978. *The Mosaics of Roman North Africa: Studies in Iconography and Patronage.* Oxford.

______. 1999. *Mosaics of the Greek and Roman World.* Cambridge.

Egloff, M. 1977. *Kellia: la poterie Copte.* Geneva.

Empereur, J.-Y. and M. Picon. 1989. "Les régions de production d'amphores impériales en Méditerranée orientale." *Anfore Romane e storia economica: un decennio di ricerche.* Collection de l'Ecole Française de Rome 114: 223–48.

______. 1998. "Les ateliers d'amphores du lac Mariut." *Bulletin de Correspondance Hellénique, Supplément* 33: 75–91.

Fraser, P.M. 1993. "Byzantine Alexandria: Decline and Fall." *Bulletin de la Sociéte Archéologique d'Alexandrie* 45: 91–106.

Geissen, A. 1978. *Katalog alexandrinischer Kaisermünzen der Sammlung des Instituts für Altertumskunde der Universität zu Köln*, II. Opladen.

Germain, S. 1969. *Les mosaïques de Timgad. Ètude descriptive et analytique.* Paris.

Gozlan, Suzanne and Ariane Bourgeois. 1992. *La maison du triomphe de Neptune à Acholla (Botria, Tunisie), Tome 1: Les mosaïques.* Collections de l'Ecole Française de Rome: 160.

Graham, J.W. 1966. Origins and interrelations of the Greek house and the Roman house. *Phoenix* 20: 3–25.

Guidobaldi, F. 1994. *Sectilia pavimenta di Villa Adriana.* Rome 1994.

Guimier-Sorbets, A.-M. 1998. "Le pavement du triclinium à la Méduse dans une maison d'époque impériale à Alexandrie." *Alexandrina* 1: 115–40.

Guimier-Sorbets, A.-M. and M.-D. Nenna. 1992. "L'emploi du verre, de la faïence et de la peinture dans les mosaïques de Délos." *Bulletin de Correspondance Hellénique* 16: 607–31.

Hayes, J.W. 1972. *Late Roman Pottery.* London.

Heinzel, H., R. Fitter., and J. Parslow. 1995. *Collins Pocket Guide: Birds of Britain and Europe with North Africa and the Middle East.* Harper-Collins (second revised edition).

Ibrahim, L., R. Scranton, and R. Brill. 1976. *Kenchreai–Eastern Port of Corinth 2. The Panels of Opus Sectile in Glass.* Leiden.

Kapitän, G. 1972. "Le anfore del relitto romano di Capo Ognina (Siracusa)." *Recherches sur les amphores romaines, MEFRA* Suppl. 10: 243–52.

———. 1961. "Schiffsfrachter antiker Baugesteiner und Architeturteile." *Kilo* 39: 276–318.

Keay, S. 1984. *Late Roman Amphorae in the Western Mediterranean. A Typology and Economic Study: The Catalan Evidence,* B.A.R. Int. Series, 136. Oxford.

Khachab, A. 1957. "Les hammams du Kom Trougah." *ASAE* 54: 117ff. pl. I.

Kołątaj, W. 1992. *Imperial Baths at Kom al-Dikka, (Alexandrie VI).* Warsaw.

Kołątaj, W. and T. Kołątaj. 1975. "Polish Excavations at Kom el Dikka in Alexandria, 1967," *Bulletin de la Sociéte Archéologique d'Alexandrie,* 43: 79–97.

Kołodziejczyk, K. 1968. "Private Roman Bath at Kom al-Dikka in Alexandria." *Études et Travaux*: 143–54.

Kraeling, C.H. 1962. *Ptolemais, City of the Libyan Pentapole.* Chicago.

Levi, D. 1947. *Antioch Mosaic Pavements,* vols. 1–2. Princeton.

Ling, R. 1991. *Roman Painting.* Cambridge: 2–22.

1998. *Ancient Mosaics.* London.

Lloyd, J.A., ed. 1978. *Excavations at Sidi Khrebish Benghazi (Berenice) vol. I. Supplement to Libya Antiqua V.* Tripoli.

MacKenzie, J. 1990. *The Architecture of Petra.* Oxford.

MacKenzie, J. 1996. "The architectural style of Roman and Byzantine Alexandria and Egypt," in D.M. Bailey, ed. *Archaeological Research in Roman Egypt. Journal of Roman Archaeology, Supplementary Series 19.* Ann Arbor.

Mahmud Bey (el-Falaki). 1872. *Mémoire sur l'antique Alexandrie.* Copenhagen.

Majcherek, G. 1992. "The late Roman ceramics from sector 'G'" (Alexandria 1986–87), *Études et Travaux* 16 (1992): 82–16.

Majcherek, G. 1995a. "Alexandria 1994: Excavations." *Polish Archaeology in the Mediterranean* 6: 11–20.

______. 1995b. "Notes on Alexandrian habitat. Roman and Byzantine houses from Kom al-Dikka." *TOPOI*, 5/1: 133–50.

______. 1995c. "Gazan Amphorae: Typology Reconsidered," in *Hellenistic and Roman Pottery in the Eastern Mediterranean, Advances in Scientific Studies*, eds. H. Meyza and J. Młynarczyk. Warsaw: 163–78.

Majcherek, G. 1998. "Kom al-Dikka, Excavations 1996–1997." *Polish Archaeology in the Mediterranean* 9: 23–36.

Marangou-Lerat, A. 1995. *Le vin et les amphores de Crète de l'époque classique à l'époque impériale*. Athens.

Michaelides, D. 1992. *Cypriot Mosaics*. Nicosia.

______. 1995. *The Pavements of Berenice. Excavations at Sidi Khrebish (Berenice)*. Vol. IV, London, 1998.

Michałowski, K. 1958. "Les fouilles polonaises a Tell Atrib," *ASAE* 58: 235–45.

Mingazzini, P. 1972. *L'insula di Giasone Magno a Cirene*. Rome.

Mosaïque 1977. *Mosaïque no 1*. Deterioration et Conservation, *ICCROM*. Rome.

______. 1983. *Mosaïque no 2*. Safeguard, Carthage 1978, Perigeux 1980, ICCROM. Rome.

Müller, H.W. 1962. "Koptische Glasintarsien mit figürlichen Darstellungen aus Antinoe/Mittelägypten." *Pantheon* 20.

Newsletter. 1992. Newsletter Chronique no 9, ICCROM. Rome, 1992.

Panella, Cl. 1973. "Appunti su uno grupo di anfore della prima, media e tarda età imperiale." *Ostia* 3. Rome: 460–633.

1986. "Oriente ed Occidente: considerazioni su alcune anfore "egee" di età imperiale a Ostia." *Bulletin de Correspondance Hellenique, Supplément* 13: 609–36.

Pensabene, P. 1985. *Marmi antichi. Problemi d'impiego, di restauro e d'identificazione*. Rome.

______. 1993. *Elementi architetonici di Alessandria e di altri siti egiziani.* Rome.

Pesce, G. 1950. *Il 'Palazzo delle Colonne' in Tolemaide di Cirenaica.* Rome.

Pieri, D. 1998, "Les importations d'amphores orientales en Gaule méridionale durant l'Antiquité tardive et le Haut-Moyen Âge (Ive-VIIe siècles après J.-C.)." SFECAG, Actes du Congrès d'Istres, 97–106. Marseille.

Riley, J.A. 1981. "The Late Bronze Age Aegean and the Roman Mediterranean: A Case for Comparison" in *Production and Distribution: A Ceramic Viewpoint* (BAR-IS 120). Oxford.

Robinson, H.S. 1959. *Pottery of the Roman Period: The Athenian Agora Chronology.*

Rodziewicz, M. 1976. "Un quartier d'habitation gréco-romain à Kôm al-Dikka." *Études et Travaux*, 9: 169–210.

______. 1984. *Les habitations romaines tardives d'Alexandrie à la lumiere des fouilles polonaises à Kôm al-Dikka, (Alexandrie III).* Warsaw.

______. 1988. "Remarks on the Domestic and Monastic Architecture in Alexandria and Surroundings," in *The Archaeology of the Nile Delta: Problems and Priorities.* Amsterdam. 267–77.

______. 1991. "Opus sectile mosaics from Alexandria nad Mareotis." *Tesserae, Festschrift für Josef Engemann, Jahrbuch für Antike und Christentum* 18: 204–14.

Saliou, C. 1994. *Les lois de bâtiments. Voisinage et habitat urbain dans l'empire romain.* Beirut.

Tkaczow, B. 1993. *The topography of ancient Alexandria.* Warsaw.

Index

Page numbers in italics refer to captions.

α-2, mosaic 25, 26, 28, 41, 43, 44, 47, 50; *24, 27, 46, 49, 50, 51, 60*
α-3, mosaic 26, 28, 34, 43, 44, 47, 52; *24, 29, 30, 32, 33, 46, 52, 53, 54, 55, 56, 57, 58, 59*
α-4, mosaic 10
α-5, mosaic 26, 34, 43, 44; *35, 36, 37, 46, 47, 59, 60, 61, 63, 64, 65, 66*
α-6, mosaic 9, 25, 26, 38, 41, 43, 44, 46, 47, 66, 71, 81; *39, 40, 45, 67, 69, 85*
α-7, mosaic 20, 25, 38, 41, 66, 70, 81; *70*
acrylic resin 48, 56, 97
Aegean 14, 21
aeration 71
African 14, 21, 25
Africana II 21
Alexandria 1, 2, 5, 13, 14, 19, 20, 26, 33, 38; *4*
Alpha 1, 9, 10, 12, 16, 19, 23, 26, 34, 78, 95; *17, 18, 22*
American Research Center in Egypt (ARCE) 2
amphorae 13, 14, 21, 23, 25; *13*
micaceous 21
animal 40, 41, 44
archaeological 1, 2, 5, 6, 9, 12, 16, 34, 73, 83
architecture 1, 5, 7, 10, 16, 18, 19, 20, 23, 45, 74, 76, 78, 79, 84, 88, 104; *75*
ashes 103, 104; *50, 61, 67*
Asia Minor 14, 21
Augustan times 25
Aurelian 21

B, Building (House) 10–12, 79, 93, 95, 96, 98; *8*
baths 6, 84
bead 38
bedding 23, 31, 43, 44, 47, 48, 50, 53, 56, 57, 58, 59, 62, 66, 68, 70, 71, 81, 84, 104; *24, 33, 54, 67*
Berenice 34
beta 9, 18
bichrome 26, 34, 38, 39, 41, 103; *27, 30, 36*
bird 37, 38, 43, 48, 59; *36, 61*
branch 41
Brock, Edwin 2
bronze 25; *25*
buds 37
buttress 93, 95, 96

Canopus 38
carpet 28, 29, 31, 37, 38, 39, 40
ceiling 88, 92, 96, 97, 98
cement 44, 45, 48, 50, 53, 57, 58, 62, 68, 70, 71, 90, 97; *6, 55*

ceramic 14, 21
charcoal *61*
circle 26, 28, 32, 39, 84
clay 18, 83; *52*
cleaning 47, 70; *70*
coarse 14, 48; *52, 58, 67*
coin 10, 14, 23, 25, 28; *25*
column 84
complex 6, 74, 76; *75*
concrete 81, 88, 89, 90, 93, 96, 98, 99; *50, 67, 87*
conservation 1, 2, 9, 10, 20, 26, 43–71, 73, 74, 78, 79, 81, 83, 85; *49, 53, 56, 59, 60, 61, 63, 64, 65, 66, 67, 69*
construction 1, 2, 9, 13, 17, 23, 33, 70, 73, 81, 90, 93, 95, 98, 99; *88, 91, 94, 95, 97, 98, 100, 101, 104*
cornice 19, 20, 84; *18*
cubiculum 19, 20, 38, 101
Cyrenaica 34
Cyrene 34

D, House 79
damp-proofing 81, 97
debris 11, 16, 20, 48, 50, 62, 83
decoration 1, 9, 10, 19, 20, 23, 16, 28, 31, 33, 34, 37, 38, 39, 40, 41, 43, 47, 57, 58, 59, 62, 66, 68, 84, 103
Diana, Theater 34
Diocletian 21, 23
al-Djem 41
Dobrowolski, Jaroslaw 3
Doric frieze 19
drainage 71, 73, 93, 101
duck 37; *63*

Early Roman 1, 7, 11, 16, 17, 20, 28, 33, 73, 74, 77, 79, 83, 84, 95; *17, 18, 80*
earthwork 81
Egyptian Antiquities Project (EAP) 2, 3
emblema 40, 41, 44, 68, 103; *45*
escarpment 9, 74, 81, 82, 88, 89, 90, 93, 96, 98, 101
excavations 5, 6, 9, 10, 16, 34, 38, 43, 46, 62, 74, 82, 83, 100
Expanded Statement of Work 93
F, Building 10, 99, 100; *8, 12, 16*
F, House 12, 33, 79
faience 38, 40, 66
filet 26, 29, 34, 35, 37, 39, 41, 103
First Pompeian (Masonry) style 23
floor 1, 2, 9, 10, 11, 13, 14, 16, 17, 19, 20, 21, 22, 23, 24, 25, 26, 28, 29, 31, 32, 33, 34, 37, 38, 41, 43, 44, 47, 52, 57, 70, 73, 74, 77, 78, 81, 82, 83, 84, 87, 90, 93, 100, 101, 104; *24, 30, 50, 52, 56, 58, 59, 61, 67, 76*
floral 44
flower 37, 40
footbridge 2, 88, 99, 100
Frog-type 14; *14*

Gaballah, Gaballah Ali 2
gallinule 37; *66*
gamma 9
gate 74, 84
Gawlikowski, Michał 2
giallo antico 32
Giasone Magno, House of 34
glass 21, 38, 44, 59, 62, 70, 74, 77, 79, 89, 92, 98, 99, 101, 104; *61*
Greco-Roman 19
guilloche 35, 44; *37*
gymnasium 84

Habitation Quarter 11
Hadrian 25, 26, 28; *25*
hederae 40, 103
Hellenistic 38
House of the Cascade 34
Huwariya 20

insula 5, 6, 74, 103
International Committee for the Conservation of Mosaics 74
iron 92, 100
Isola Sacra 41

kantharos 37
Kapitän II 21
Kellia 14
kitchenware 14
Kołątaj, Wojciech 2
Kom al-Dikka 1, 2, 5, 20, 33, 38, 73, 74; *4, 7*

L2, street 6
lacuna 33, 44, 47, 48, 50, 53, 56, 59, 62, 68, 71, 103; *51, 55*

lamp 10, 14; *14*
landscaping 1, 2, 74
leaves 18, 37
lime 23, 24, 25, 48, 50, 56, 57, 58, 62, 68, 70, 71, 90, 104; *24, 50, 52, 58, 61, 67*
limestone 13, 17, 19, 21, 32, 37, 83, 84, 90; *18, 67*

Majcherek, Crzegorz 2
marble 13, 31, 32, 33, 37, 44, 48, 50, 53, 56, 57, 58, 59, 68, 104; *50, 58, 61, 67*
Mareotic 21
Marina al-Alamein 20
Mauritanian 21
Mediterranean 2, 14, 16, 21
Mons Porphyrites 19
monuments 5
mortar 16, 43, 44, 45, 48, 50, 52, 53, 56, 57, 58, 59, 62, 66, 68, 70, 71, 83, 90, 97, 98, 103; *52, 58, 67*
mosaic 1, 2, 9–12, 16, 17, 19–21, 23–26, 28, 29, 31, 32, 33, 34, 37, 38, 41, 43, 44–48, 50, 52, 53, 56, 57, 59, 62, 66, 68, 70, 71, 73, 74, 77, 78, 79, 81–3, 84, 87, 88, 90, 93, 96, 99, 101, 103, 104; *24, 27, 29, 30, 32, 33, 35, 36, 37, 39, 40, 45, 46, 49, 50, 51, 52, 53, 54, 55, 56, 57, 58, 59, 60, 61, 63, 64, 65, 66, 67, 69, 70, 85, 96*
Mradny, Assam 2
Mustapha Pasha, tombs of 20

Napoleonic era 5
niche 46, 81, 93, 95, 96, 97; *82, 85, 94, 95, 97, 98*
Nile silt fabric 14, 21
Nile Valley 21
North African 21
nucleus 101; *50, 61, 67*
oikos 20, 104
opus isodomum 17, 104
opus sectile 21, 25, 26, 28, 29, 31, 32, 34, 43, 44, 47, 52, 57, 58, 84, 104; *32, 33, 56, 58, 59*
opus tesselatum 23, 26, 28, 52, 84, 104
opus vermiculatum 41
Ostia 41

Palazzo delle Colonne 34
panel 20, 26, 31, 33, 34, 35, 37, 38, 39, 40, 41, 43, 44, 47, 48, 59, 62, 71, 77, 79, 81, 89, 92, 98, 99, 103; *36, 61, 63, 64, 65, 66*
panther 41, 44, 68; *45, 85*
Parandowska, Ewa 2
park 2, 73
parrot 37; *63*
pavilion 84
paving 84
pavonazzetto 32
peacock 37; *64*
Pergamon 38
peristyle 20, 104
pigeon 37; *64, 65*
platform 78, 90, 92, 100
Plextol 48, 50, 56, 58, 68
Polish Center of Mediterranean Archaeology in Cairo 2
Polish Centre of Archaeology 2, 5
Polish-Egyptian Preservation Mission 2
Polychrome 34, 35, 38
pomegranates 37, 40
porphyry 32
Portico, Theater 6, 28, 84
pottery 10, 14, 103; *16, 22, 67*
preservation 1, 2, 45, 46
Proconessian 32
pseudo-peristyle 20
Ptolemaic 18, 19
Ptolemais 34

quail 37; *65*

R4, street 6, 9, 74, 84, 101, *75*
R5, street 6
reconstruction 31, 45, 47, 48, 62, 68, 83, 84; *45, 51, 57, 80*
Red Slip 14
removal 12, 16, 38, 45, 48, 70, 81; *80*
repairs 33, 41, 44, 45, 48, 53, 57, 62
Rodziewicz, M. 11, 23, 34
Roman/Byzantine 5, 6, 7, 9, 10, 11, 12, 13, 74, 76, 77, 79, 81, 83, 89, 90, 93, 95, 96, 98, 99; *8, 11, 12, 14, 16*
roof 46, 59, 74, 76, 77, 81, 88, 89, 90–93, 96, 101; *88, 91*
rosso antico 32

rubble 94, 104; *24, 52, 58*
rudus 102; *24, 50, 52, 58, 67*
ruins 7, 9, 20, 21, 74, 76, 84, 88

Safiya Zaghloul Street 9, 76, 84
sand 48, 58, 68, 70, 104; *50, 52, 58, 61*
semis 28, 102; *30*
setting bed 48, 62, 104; *50, 52, 58, 61, 67*
sewage 13, 101
shelter 1, 2, 46, 73, 74, 76, 79, 81, 84, 87–100; *6, 75, 76, 77, 78, 82, 85*
Sigillata, Eastern 25
similes 14
soil 44, 59, 68, 71, 101; *67*
square 6, 9, 19, 26, 28, 29, 32, 33, 34, 35, 37, 38, 39, 40, 41, 44, 68, 76, 84, 103
staircase 84
statumen 104; *58, 61, 67*
steel 76, 88, 90, 92, 99, 100, 101
stone 11, 20, 21, 22, 37, 43, 44, 48, 52, 57, 62, 83, 92, 93, 97, 98, 103, 104; *24, 50, 58, 61, 67*
Styrofoam 77, 92
sub-Koan 25
Supreme Council of Antiquities (SCA) 2, 3, 73

Tell Atrib 20
tendrils 40
terminus post quem 25
tesserae 68, 71, 103, 104; *67*
textile 70
Thmuis 38
tourist attraction 2
Trajan 25; *25*
tree 41, 99
triangle 32, 40, 84
triclinia 28, 33
triclinium 19, 20, 22, 25, 31, 34, 83, 84, 100, 104; *30*
Tripolitanian III 21
truss 76, 77, 90, 92, 101; *91*

United States Agency for International Development (USAID) 2
Utica 34

vegetal ornament 40
vessel 13, 14, 21, 25
Via Canopica 6
Villa 1, 7, 9, 10, 12, 16, 17, 19, 23, 26, 34, 43, 77, 78, 81–84, 95, 100; *18, 22*
Villa of the Birds 9, 38
Vincent, Robert K. 2

wall 10, 11, 12, 14, 16–23, 28, 29, 39, 43, 44, 46, 48, 52, 59, 62, 70, 74, 77, 78, 79, 81–84, 88, 89, 90, 92, 93–100; *8, 24, 80*
wooden 20, 77, 92, 100; *78*
workshop 81, 90